WHISPERS OF AN OLD SOUL

ROMAN GARREIS

ANAPHORA LITERARY PRESS

QUANAH, TEXAS

Anaphora Literary Press
1108 W 3rd Street
Quanah, TX 79252
https://anaphoraliterary.com

Book design by Anna Faktorovich, Ph.D.

Copyright © 2018 by Roman Garreis

All rights reserved. No part of this book may be reproduced in any form or by any electronic or mechanical means, including information storage and retrieval systems, without permission in writing from Roman Garreis. Writers are welcome to quote brief passages in their critical studies, as American copyright law dictates.

Printed in the United States of America, United Kingdom and in Australia on acid-free paper.

Edited by: Elizabeth Coletti

Published in 2018 by Anaphora Literary Press

Whispers of an Old Soul
Roman Garreis—1st edition.

Library of Congress Control Number: 2018947762

Library Cataloging Information

Garreis, Roman, author.
    Whispers of an old soul / Roman Garreis
    298 p. ; 9 in.
    ISBN 978-1-68114-439-9 (softcover : alk. paper)
    ISBN 978-1-68114-440-5 (hardcover : alk. paper)
    ISBN 978-1-68114-441-2 (e-book)
1. Poetry—Subjects & Themes—Nature. 2. Poetry—American—General.
3. Poetry—Subjects & Themes—Love & Erotica.
PN6099-6110: Collections of general literature: Poetry
811: American poetry in English

Whispers of an Old Soul

ROMAN GARREIS

TABLE OF CONTENTS

Peacefully Entangled	10
Inflamed Heart	11
Embracing this Space	12
Ambiences	13
Love's Embrace	14
Existent	15
Barefoot Girl	16
Two Hearts	17
Blessed	18
Caregivers	19
Child of Vastness	20
Ambience of Love	21
In Faraway Eyes	22
Whispers	23
When Love Comes	24
Always Nice to See You	25
The Blur of Forever	26
Fading Tears	27
I Just Know	28
Embracing Eternity	29
Companion	30
Our Souls Singing in the Night	31
A Wife	32
No More Wishes	33
One and Only	34
A Lover a Partner a Very Close Friend	35
Side-by-Side	36
Monday through Friday Blues	37
Tender Moments	38
Eyes Wide Open	39
Reason	40
Nothing Less than my Life	41
In the Way	42
Just One Thought	43
One Winter Day	44
this love (part 1)	45
Faithfully	46
Never to Another	47
this love (part 2)	48
Searching	49
If I Could Fly	50
As You Left	51
Should I Ever	52
Uncontrolled Emotion	53
Heaven Seems so Far Away Now	54
The Passing Years	55
Together Forever	56
Waiting on Dreams	57
Quintessence	58
Glorious Allure	59
Intertwined	60
With Love to You	61
Words	62
Unlearning the Lesson	63
Passing Moments	64
Creation of a Star	65
I, Butterfly	66
Nearing the End	67
Gypsy Woman	68
From Within	69
Where I Always Want to Be	70
In the End	71
Drizzle with a Little Sprinkle	72
Journey	73
Lost	74
Mannish Man	75
Making You Appear	76
Rainy Day Girl	77
Poetic Hugs	78
Precious Gift	79
Precious	80
Silk and Feathers	81
So Far Away Yet So Close	82
Tears	83
Words of Love	84
Free to Soar	85
Promises Promises	86
Emergent of Self	87
The Journey Within	88
Waves of Joy	89
The Warmth of Her	90
Precious You	91
Unimaginable	92
Transcending to Me	93
Growing Pains	94
In Time of Need	95
Could See Forever	96
Facing the Day	97
The Disguise	98
So Silly	99
So Rare	100
In the Shadow of Her	101

Perfect Stranger	102	Before	152
Nowhere to Go	103	Omnipresence	153
Waiting	104	To Hear You	154
In Passing	105	Fading Away	155
As Tears Fall	106	Driven to Tears	156
A Beautiful Secret	107	Enraptured	157
Purple	108	Never Before	158
Unambiguous	109	The Blessing	159
Between the Words	110	Beyond the Stare	160
Stay	111	Naked	161
Sacred Love	112	From Within Love	162
One Wonderful Day	113	Beautiful As You	163
In the Silence of Me	114	Unbreakable Spirit	164
Falling	115	We Fall	165
In a Friend's Hand	116	Respectful Awe	166
Deific Light	117	Parasol	167
Angel of Bliss	118	Versions of Me	168
Caged	119	The Wanting	169
You Came	120	Life	170
I Breathe	121	Vivacious Verve	171
Surrender	122	The Journey	172
Touching	123	The Silence of Love	173
Emergent Youth	124	In the Shadows	174
In My Darkest Night	125	Broken Heartbeat	175
Dissipating Haze	126	That Someone	176
A Song Unsung	127	Our Little Angel	177
Transcendent Love	128	Ray of Sunshine	178
Sharing Thoughts	129	September	179
Radiance	130	The Peace of One	180
Such Are Things	131	Playful	181
Smiling Heart	132	The Strength to Cry	182
Fornication	133	Waiting on a Friend	183
Seeing the Light	134	Hopefully Waiting	184
Beyond the Morning Light	135	A Million Tears (2)	185
Beautifully One	136	A Million Tears (1)	186
Lifting the Mask	137	The Hero Within	187
The Wide Open Door	138	The Here of Lost Love	188
As I Woke to You	139	Stand	189
Impassioned Scream	140	Alone	190
From Within the Light	141	Caring Arms Of	191
End of Ends	142	Brown Sugar	192
Hit and Run	143	Tiny Songbirds	193
Play Play Play	144	Freefalling into Emptiness	194
Until You	145	Inimitable Love	195
Brave Volunteer	146	Grateful Surrender	196
Feeling Words	147	In the Light of a New Day	197
In Your Eyes	148	Shadow	198
Dreaming a Dream	149	To This I Give	199
Silent Hurt	150	I Want	200
Nowhere Fast	151	Blessed Be	201

Illuminating Care	202
Essence of Love	203
Introspective Love	204
Seeing Me	205
Within Love's Sleep	206
Running to You	207
Embracing Each Other	208
Fanning the Flames	209
Morning After Beautiful	210
Sweet Caress	211
Nothing Came	212
God and Goddess	213
Scars	214
Wholeheartedly Yours	215
All of a Sudden	216
Sands of Time	217
Silent Love	218
As I Made My Wish	219
Angelic Warrior	220
Awakened to Us	221
Light of Love	222
Wish	223
Between There and Here	224
The You to Me	225
As You Give	226
Lifetime After Never	227
Glimpse	228
Dare to Love	229
A Love So True	230
As One	231
Emptiness	232
Breathtaking	233
So Very Big	234
Edge of Frenzy	235
Falling Away from Me	236
Freely Yours	237
Glory of Love	238
Glow	239
Calling Her Names	240
Blessings	241
In the Sorrow of Nothingness	242
One Moment Too Long	243
Longing	244
Our of the Blue	245
Immersed	246
Enchanting	247
Heaven Above	248
Darkness	249
Enchanted Room	250
Emotional Touch	251
As One Soul	252
Forever	253
Love, Laugh and Play	254
Love Eternal	255
Hugs and Kisses	256
No More Wishes	257
I Promise	258
In My Whispers	259
Captivating Magic	260
Ropes of Steel	261
Forever Us	262
Depth of Love	263
Rush of Joy	264
Through a Rainbow	265
Wildfire	266
Like a Dream	267
Eternal Love	268
Serenity	269
Waiting	270
Shades of Pink	271
The Thought of You	272
Wonderful Love	273
So Deep Asleep	274
All of Me	275
Promises	276
In Massive Awe	277
Such a Woman	278
Beyond Heartbreak	279
No Cure	280
Back to Her	281
Within Forever	282
A Wonderful Thing	283
Children Playing	284
Unconquerably One	285
Empathic	286
Breathing into You	287
On My Way (to me)	288
Beyond Unsure	289
Your Touch	290
Upon My Love	291
Adoring Awe	292
Within the Space Between	293
Light Within the Dark	294
So in Love	295
Ripped Clothes	296
Muse	297

There is nothing more wonderful and beautiful in this life than to be surrounded by the divine sacred feminine energy. To be so is emotionally enriching and a true celebration of living. In its true essence and at the very depths of its core is the warmth of love and compassion that nurtures a happiness and soulful harmony which can be felt nowhere else. I thank you all for engulfing my heart, soul and being within the magnificence and glory of its interminable light. You each are a goddess to behold and cherish.

I will develop myself in a positive manner and avoid anything that may reduce my mental, emotional and spiritual growth or my physical health. I will develop self-discipline in order to help bring out the best in myself and others. I will use common sense and never be abusive or offensive. I am dedicated. I am motivated. I am on a quest to be at one within love of all.

Dedicated to those who hear the whispers.

Peacefully Entangled

All my illusions are real
Each one intertwined within everything I feel
From the unicorns and dragons that my spirit ride
To that place where all of the pixies, fairies, elves
and leprechauns reside

It is all from within a place of peace
Where the fun and laughter never seems to cease
As everyone and everything there wishes never ever to be elsewhere
As we each so happily play without even a care

So if it looks at times like I am lost and in a daze
Or cannot be found for days and days
Know that everything is okay
As I am in a place where I am just waiting for you to come and play

Inflamed Heart

I express
That which I so passionately caress
That which makes me laugh and cry
That which is envisioned by the sight of my third eye

I do so with love and care
As easy as I breathe the air
As to provoke a feeling that might have never been before
To inflame the fire of the heart to burn bright forever more

This brings me happiness
A soulful sense of bliss
That it is I who have answered this call
To share that which touches the depth of the soul with all

Embracing this Space

There are witches here
Who share their energy without fear
And here there are some gypsies too
Who understand the fortunes in all that we do

And here are some religious women of belief
Holding us all so tight in our need of relief
And here are so many intuitive women who are guiding the way
So that we all know deep within our hearta that all is okay

And here are heaven sent souls
Angelic women who care for us all in whole
As we all are right here sharing this precious space
Within the loving protection of each other's embrace

Ambiences

I vibrate
Within the frequency of 528
A tone that resonates within everything everywhere
For all to embrace and somehow share

It is a frequency that engulfs the very essence of all that is and will ever be
A harmonic vibration that was created long before the apple and the tree
That brings transformation and miracles into our existence
To connect hearts no matter how far the distance

Such a beautiful state of being to be in
That lifts the divine soul from deep within
For it is the sound of peace and harmony
A sacred place where love will always be

Love's Embrace

I love love
Which I embrace every little bit of
For I am so captivated by it all no matter what kind
Intimate, friendship, family or even blind

So much that I seek it everywhere I go
From everyone that I do and do not know
For sharing the feeling fills the depths of my heart and soul
As the energy of it utterly and completely engulfs me in whole

There is truly just nothing like it
The bliss of feeling it take over my entire being bit-by-bit
As I unconsciously start to adjust
From the cautious distance of the mind to the hopeful heartfelt
      feeling of unconditional trust

Just all so powerful
The moment just all so beautiful
How when it is a gentle love it brings so much comfort in every way
And when it is an intense passionate love how it uncontrollably takes
      my breath away

Just so unpredictable and rare
Which with all my heart with all I will forever share
As I wish this wonderful feeling for everyone everywhere
As easy as I breathe the life giving air

Existent

Live through each moment
In the way that you feel each was sent
With each and every one and everything there
Being all so very special and rare

Let it amaze you to the very depths of your soul
Make you feel complete and whole
With intense passion and zest
It all being a part of a wonderful quest

Let it bring you joy
Be everything that you enjoy
With no heaviness of past sorrow
Or anticipation of what it all may bring tomorrow

Barefoot Girl

Untamed wild and free
A rousing vision for all to see
As she dances joyously barefoot in the grass
As the moments slowly fall through the hole of the hourglass

Such a girly girl this barefoot girl
As precious as a rare pearl
With such a bright light beaming from deep within her soul
With no sense of her ever being under someone's control

Casting images between what is fantasy and what is real
With such a vibrant energy for all to feel
Oh wild barefoot girl please let us dance with you
As we may all be engulfed within the enchantments of all that you do

Two Hearts

She truly cares a lot
For everything from an animal to a tot
Today she saw a bird trying to land on a rope
And went over to give it some hope

The bird did not fly away
As she gave it love in her own special way
It just choose another place to land
As it flew to her outreached hand

They both looked into each other's souls
With the belief that they could trust each other in whole
As for one special moment of cheer
Two special hearts beat together without fear

Blessed

She is a bright star
That can be seen from afar
Caring so much about another
Wanting only happiness for the other

So wonderful this woman of love
Blessed by the lord above
For her heart bleeds for those in life pain
Giving all that she can without the thought of what's to gain

She is as special as anyone can be
Above all else who try to be
For her to call you a friend
Means to have someone by your side until the bitter end

Caregivers

They are more special than a white rose
With an inner beauty that just grows and grows
With a smile so precious and true
They are the essence of love through and through

With the grace of an angel in flight
They touch hearts with the caring energy of love's light
Bringing to those they touch peace of soul
Filling up what once was an empty hole

It is special how they just do this with so much care
How those around them just smile the moment they are there
For within them is the spirit of a God-given gift indeed
The heart and soul of being a precious caregiver to those in need

Child of Vastness

I believe in everything
In the power of positive and negative energies and all that each will
        bring
In the peace of soul in speaking the words "In Goddess I Trust"
In the magic of the sprinkling of fairy dust

I believe in it all
In the harmony of all before the fall
In the emotional healing from looking into a smiling face
That there is something in the space between space

I believe unconditionally
In the power of channeling the universal energy
In the intelligent existence as close as on Jupiter or Mars
And that everything and anything is possible within the vastness
        beyond the stars

Ambience of Love

I can feel its lure
Into what feels so pure
This magnificent energy of collective love
Which surrounds me from within without below and above

This I embrace
As it fills within me my empty space
With colors imagery and sound
Which within it can only be found

And so it is with all of my heart and mind
That I leave the body of me behind
Where to within the vibrations of such a beautiful energy
I release my soul to soar free

In Faraway Eyes

On our way
To where we just cannot say
To that of which is unknown
Beyond all of what is already known

Not knowing where or when
With memories of where we've been
Our direction set by the stars above
As carefree as a high-flying dove

We were born to roam
We call everywhere our home
As some say this all comes at a cost
Where we say not all those who wander are lost

Whispers

I woke this morning with you next to me
The thought pierced my heart that this was always
where I wanted to be
Immediately a calmness came over my mind
All the good of life suddenly I could find

I lay there letting the joy rush through my soul
Could feel the lightness of my body as my happiness
lifted me in whole
The secrets of life all at my command
As I intensified the moment by touching your hand

You moved and my excitement uncontrollably started to soar
Every bit of my existence began to embarrassingly roar
And as my passion began to lead my way
I whispered these words to you… I love you more
each and every day

When Love Comes

When love comes it comes with determination and power
When it comes it comes to devour
When love is felt it asks for no reason
When it wants to be it waits for no season

Sunshine shines bright on those who love
Angels sing for them from high above
Joy in everything when it is shared by two
Nothing impossible for them to do

Love is just such a magical kind of thing
Brings such magnificent meaning to the experience of everything
And truthfully speaking from the bottom of my soul
Once felt, without it you will never again feel whole

Always Nice to See You

The soaring of a dove
Two people in love
The rise of the morning sun
Playful kids having fun

Stars twinkling in the night
A long flowing tail of a high-flying kite
The trees the flowers and the bees
The graceful ships upon the seas

The deep colors of an autumn day
A misty shower in the month of May
The images through a morning dew
And the wonderful sight of every bit of you

The Blur of Forever

Since you have been gone
I lie awake in my bed beyond dawn
Without so much as a desire to rise
Feeling only darkness within each new sunrise

And as my empty hours pass by
I find only the strength to cry
For I am so lost and alone
Struggling to now face each moment on my own

Not even sure when it is that I took my last breath
No difference between the feeling of life and death
All just a faded blur within a blur
As I now let go of us forever

Fading Tears

Contemplating the exact second of my demise
Dreading the moment of another mournful sunrise
Arguing with fate of how he was so wrong
Finding myself lost to where I belong

Really feeling beaten down by the heaviness of that around me
Blinded by the sight of the misery I now have to see
Engulfed in the pain of so many heartbreaking tears
Consumed by the reality of my hidden fears

Feeling the bleakness of each and every day
When out of nowhere you came my way
Now I have found in me the reason to cope
For your simple compassion and gentleness has brought me so much
    hope

I Just Know

I am told of a place that has the brightest light
Of a place where I will one day take my angelic flight
Told of the peace and harmony that is waiting there
Told of the happiness that I will share

Told that it is a place without pain or sorrow
A place without worriment of tomorrow
A place that has a forever sunrise
A place far beyond my demise

I am told it is a place that will surpass all of my fantasies
A place full of wonderment as far as I can see
But deep in my heart I know that this place will be no more than this
Than the feeling I have in the love of your kiss

Embracing Eternity

No love compares to ours
It surpasses all by far
Nothing will change it or make it wrong
What we have will remain forever strong

It will cause our souls to never die
Through the heavens it will help us to fly
And with the joy of God's given grace
Eternity it will help us to embrace

In comparison, Romeo and Juliet's slightly fairs
An underestimation to exclaim of it being so rare
But not because of the love that I have for you or you for me
But because it is all that a love should truly be

Companion

You are the reason for my creation
The hope for my salvation
My soul lives and will never die
Because of the love of you and I

For when I look into your eyes I see another day
When I'm lost in my direction you show me the way
My life was a moment and you made it an eternity
Was unfulfilled and you filled it with all that could ever be

So to you my soul I do extend
To be yours with no sense of an end
So there may never be a never
With you as my companion now and forever

Our Souls Singing in the Night

I woke to witness our souls engulfed in each other's arms
To see them so happy to be so far from harm
They circled my room like children at play
With mine always leading but yours showing the way

I lay there in fear as together they started to part
Did not know how to feel as their departure pierced my heart
But then your soul turned to me with its face all a glow
To assure me that they were happy no matter where they might go

But still I wondered what they were going to do
If they could keep their happiness that they were so rightly due
Till suddenly I felt their joy so deep in my heart
For I could hear them sing as they swore never to part

A Wife

A wife is someone I wish to be with through each and every season
Someone I want to be with for no apparent reason
Someone who causes me to feel comfort through all my unease
Someone whom I can feel in a calm summer's breeze

A wife is someone I sense deep in my heart
Someone I mourn whenever we part
Someone who sets my spirit free from the bonds of my earthly
    restrain
Someone who makes me feel like my emotions are on a runaway train

A wife is someone I taste within the early morning dew
Someone I feel free to give the depths of my innocence to
Someone who offers me the feeling of a true love
Someone I can see in the flight of a soaring dove

A wife is someone who I behold all of my future in
Someone who is where all of my memories begin
Someone who is to me more than a dream come true
Someone whom I find in no one else but you

No More Wishes

She has always been in all of my dreams
Her image I see in the brightness of a moon beam
She captured my soul possesses my heart
My love for her was everything right from the start

She is all I ever think of
All I ever thought was love
The moments with her so exquisite
Of her I love every little bit

I have no future know no past
My life is in this moment that I want to forever last
For now I have all I ever wished for
I have her and need not wish no more

One and Only

You are the one
The light of my sun
The moon beam in the night
The strength of a victorious knight

You are alone in stance
Heaven at a glance
The one who brings meaning to lifelong
The inspiration to a love song

You are the one and only
The triumph over lonely
You are who you are
No better love for me by far

A Lover a Partner a Very Close Friend

Sometimes you can see it coming from afar
Sometimes it passes you like a shooting star
It is something that you are really never ready for
Something that always changes the way you were before

It is the spark that creates a raging fire
The fierce force behind passion and desire
A feeling that causes your spirit to soar high in the sky
A memory that brings a tear to your eye

It is love which is such a very strange thing
For you never know what it might bring
A lover a partner a very close friend
A deep down feeling that will stay with you until the very end

Side-by-Side

We were meant to be here and meant to go far
It is who we were, who we will be and who we are
Sadness to happiness from one moment to the soon after
One split second of tears and the next laughter

Side-by-side through things of which we know and know not
Embracing the joys that overshadow the pains that tie us in a knot
Each day the twists and turns making it all so rough
Nevertheless, each glance at each other assuring that it will never be too tough

So much in love so much of life so much to understand
So much thought of why we hold each other's hand
All in an existence that was meant to be
In a love and life shared by the creation of you and me

Monday through Friday Blues

Monday, and I just left your side
And from my sadness I have nowhere to hide
Tuesday, no better than the day before
In fact I think it hurts that much more

Wednesday, I'm trying hard to find a way to cope
But suffer even deeper when I realize for this there is no hope
Thursday, and I pray that I will soon start to feel alright
But the tears keep right on flowing well into the night

Friday, afraid to even make a sound
Spent the whole day on the verge of a nervous breakdown
For the week is so long when I do not have you
For whenever I am without you I just do not know what to do

Tender Moments

There is a secret place where my woman and I go
A place of which only she and I know
It is a place with flowers and trees
A place where she shares her happiness with me

It is a place where we sit by a lake
And promise each other that our love we will never forsake
It is a place where we enjoy every moment of a day
A place where I wish we could forever stay

It is a place that has the freshness of the morning dew
A place which leaves us in the wanting of nothing else to do
It is a place where we walk hand in hand
A place where we talk and make our plans

It is a place where the moments pass too fast
A place where we wish the day would eternally last
It is a place that we love so much
A place where our hearts first learned to touch

Eyes Wide Open

I am dreaming with my eyes wide open
And never to wake is what I am hoping
For I am moved as much as any one person can
By the very thought of me being your man

For your love for me is so overwhelmingly real
My heart I give to you in hope that our life together it will seal
For you are a woman of so many emotional treasures
A woman with the ability to cause me so many wonderful pleasures

And it is all so clear to me right now
That all I live for is you somehow
For our love to me is everlastingly true
For I feel no love without the love of you

Reason

Life brought us together
Gave me a feeling of us forever
That all that would be would be forever strong
That with you all would never be wrong

But now it tries so hard to keep us apart
Puts this heavy burden upon my heart
Which has left me wondering why it must be
What is the reason for the loneliness of you and me

When all I can do is sit here in total thought
Totally worn out from the battle that my emotions have fought
In another moment that I must suffer through
Without the precious presence of you

Nothing Less than my Life

It is not fair to love a person as much as this
And not even be able to share so much as a kiss
Leaves me lonely so empty inside
Causes my happiness to run and hide

It is for me all so very sad
To think of yesterday of what it was that we had
The smiling the kissing the good times we spent
The joy of feeling that to each other we are content

It all seems so very wrong
To part from her love that feels so strong
To not think of her as my life
To think of her as anything other than my wife

In the Way

In the way that you look in the sun
In the way that we have fun
In the way of the things you say
In the way that we so playfully play

In the way that you care for all
In the way that you make me feel ten feet tall
In the way that we love
In the way that I know you came from the lord above

In the way that you so gently touched my heart
In the way that this was right right from the start
In the way that you do all that you do
Is in the way that I love you

Just One Thought

I felt so empty today
Felt my soul quickly fade away
All of my insignificance came to mind
My spirit I could no longer find

My breath was no longer within the lungs of me
My existence throbbed in immense agony
My legs no longer would help me to walk
My voice was no longer a partner for me to talk

My every emotion totally touched
Everything that I am was entirely crushed
I felt my whole life coming to an end
No longer the reason to reason could I comprehend

Everything about me was coming apart
No longer could I feel the beating of my heart
All I knew was that I was ready to die
Just because I thought about you saying good-bye

One Winter Day

Songs of peace and happiness
Only increased my sadness
Even the excitement within the children
Had no effect on the state of mind I was in

So much that I did not enjoy the twinkling lights
Did not even enjoy the season sights
Even when the snow fell I did not smile
Only felt the tears of my loneliness the whole while

Presents all around but I did not care
Sharing within the giving spirit I could not bear
For my one wish did not come true
That the blessings of this one winter day could have been shared with you

this love

(part 1)

this love has gone crazy
has taken over every part of me
controls the very essence of me
allows only of it for me to see
causes me to know soulful misery
shows me no emotional pity
sends my mind wondering like a refugee
drills my decisions with the third degree
permits only to it my ecstasy
creates a lock on all of my abilities with it as the only key
manipulates all that I'll ever be
to everything it wants I agree
leaves my soul in complete debris
makes my life feel like a catastrophe
causes me to beg for compassion from my knees
rules my life with no uncertainty
provokes the fire of my jealousy
is stronger than my will times three
has my feelings committing total anarchy
holds my heart in emotional captivity
knows that I am now an emotional casualty
entirely consumes all of my mental energy
limits my comprehensibility
beats me up with consistency
manipulates all of my decency
alters my individuality
threatens my emotional sanity
holds me in soulful slavery
abuses me without sympathy
is to me a complete mystery
over me claims victory

Faithfully

It is the way you love me that has captured my heart
The way I treasure that love that has helped this
relationship to start
It is my heart to you I will always send
For it is the way that you caress me that will never let
me let us end

It is your sensitivity for me that I will always cherish
And it is this that I will do until my life has completely perished
Full with complete anticipation of you taking
my feelings to a level that is so very much higher
The truth of the matter is, my life is completely engulfed
by the ecstasy of your desires

My every breath is made only because of your existence
And it is to my very essence that this will always be
without resistance
For now my life is no longer mine to live
For it is forever to you that my life I now faithfully give

Never to Another

Take my sight
So I may never see in another
What I have seen in her

Take my hands
So I may never touch another
Like I have touched her

Take my feelings
So I may never feel for another
Like I feel for her

Take away everything I am for her
So I may never be anything to another

Take away this all from me
If you ever decide
To take her away from me

this love

(part 2)

this love is to me an emotional necessity
causes me to feel forever free
allows me to lie with no one but thee
causes me to feel a soulful glee
balances my life with harmony
will always be with honesty
motivates my emotional curiosity
enhances my spiritual tranquility
caresses me all so tenderly
is a fulfillment of my ultimate fantasy
is the deepest part of my memory
is something I'll always want as my reality
will always have my complete loyalty
will always be the greatest part of my emotional journey
is written by poets in their soulful poetry
is a love that will be with me throughout my eternity
was always meant as part of my destiny

Searching

I searched the streets for it yesterday
And in the alleys before that day
And last night I hit all the bars
While afterward checking all the passing cars

Then I looked for it at one of the cafes
As I watched all the people carrying the trays
And one time I even thought I found it in my bed
But in the morning found that I had been extremely misled

And just as my hopes started to fade
Just when I gave up belief in the prayers I prayed
Just when I thought that I could search no more
I found you and the love I was searching for

If I Could Fly

Oh butterfly, oh butterfly so high in the sky
Oh how like you I wish I could fly
For I would fly away with my heart in my hand
For it's my heart that bleeds all over this land

I would fly and I would fly until I was way out of sight
I'd fly through the day and all through the night
I would fly over the ocean and straight through her door
I would fly to the woman whom my heart is now bleeding for

And I'd give her my love, my happiness, and my joy
Until again my tenderness she could enjoy
Oh butterfly, oh butterfly so high in the sky
Oh how like you I wish I could fly

As You Left

A tear fought its way to my eye
As I watched you so sadly wave good-bye
And as you faded from my view
I remained there lost not knowing what to do

After a few moments with nothing to say
I somehow found the strength to walk away
Only to feel the pain strike deep in my heart
As the breathtaking thought came that we were now apart

The emptiness took hold
As my knees began to buckle and fold
As I made my way through the mob
As I tried so hard not to stop and sob

Now here I am
Feeling as if I have been hit by a battering ram
As the world goes on with life
As I agonized over the moments apart from my precious wife

Should I Ever

Should I say good-bye if she ever breaks my heart
Or would not my heart break more if we were to part
Should I say good-bye if she ever causes me sadness
Or would this not take away what was left of my happiness

Should I say good-bye if I did not like what she had to say
Or would I not feel totally empty without hearing her words everyday
Should I say good-bye if she makes me feel like I am not the only one
Or would I not lose everything I am if she were not there when my day was done

Should I say good-bye if her eyes ever became cold towards me
Or would I not beg God to take my vision if it were her eyes that I could no longer see
Should I say good-bye if it were her touch I enjoyed no more
Or would I miss the chance that she may touch me again like she did before

Should I say good-bye if she ever causes me to cry
Or would not the loss of her cause me to live the rest of my life within a sigh
Should I say good-bye if I ever had any reason to say good-bye
Or would not the reason be the reason that I would just lay down and die

Uncontrolled Emotion

Why can't I search past what I think I see
Past this emotion called jealousy
Maybe it's because she is much too beautiful for me
Or maybe I'm just too much in fear of my insecurities

Why can't I understand that her love is only for me
Why can't I understand that without her my life is so empty
Why can't I feel what her love means to me
Why can't I control this feeling that now controls me

Why can't I control this rage I feel so deep in my heart
Why don't I understand that if I do not my life will soon fall apart
How strange that this small emotion causes me to feel so much hate
Just hope that it does not tear down everything that we try to create

Pray that one day this feeling will all go away
Pray it leaves without leaving me a price to pay
Pray that one day I break down and see
That her love was always meant just for me

Heaven Seems so Far Away Now

Please tell me everything will be alright
I need something to hold on to in order to make it through this night
For it is another night that I will be on my own
Now that I am here all alone

It is all like being part of an empty shattered dream
Leaving me without the strength to even let out a scream
Just to wake seems like a complete waste to do
Underestimation to just say that I feel so emotionally blue

And no matter where it is that I go
The memory of me being with you is all that I now know
And with long deep breaths each being longer than the other
I wait for death without you as my lover

And with my soul no longer able to soar
I no longer feel peace without you to adore
And with each moment passing with no apparent reason
I can feel the slowness of each agonizing season

And no matter what I do I find myself unable to cope
Find myself lost and without hope
For the ending of us will never feel right
For you were always my reason to see heaven's light

The Passing Years

Here it is again, that time of the year
The time when it's just a little harder to fight back even a single tear
When all through the day there is a whisper of all is right
That attacks my loneliness well into the night

It really doesn't matter how strong I try to be
The battle is all lost to my misery
For it knows there is no true happiness without you by my side
Knows there is nowhere for my emptiness to hide

For it is in the pureness of the snow
In the excitement of everyone joyfully on the go
In the words of those who sing a winter wonderland song
That I feel that to be without you is all so wrong

Together Forever

Let's get married and leave this world behind
Let's spend our life together in heart, soul and mind
Let's find a home that's not known to the rest
Let's give our love all of our best

Let's share our feelings that we have only for each other
Let's nurture our love that we have for one another
Let's search our emotions through all of the day and night
Let's pray that we will still do this even after the end of our life's light

Let us do it now and let us do it eternally
Let's do it as part of our destiny
Let's do all it is that we do for us two
Let's do it together, just me and you

Waiting on Dreams

Woke this morning looking for you
Not quite sure of where I was or what to do
Felt so empty so confused so out of place
To wake and not see the beauty within your face

Was it really time to face another day
Wish I never saw the morning's ray
Really could not find the will
To do anything more than to just lie there still

So I rolled over and went back to sleep
Because that's where all the dreams of us I keep
And there I'll sleep until my dreams come true
Until that one day when I wake next to you

Quintessence

You are wonderful feelings I have never felt
Beautiful smells that I have never before smelt
Amazing colors I have never seen
Everything near and far and everything in between

You are the essence of everything lovely
All sight that I ever want to see
A mesmerizing sound that I always wanted to hear
The reason to no longer fear the feeling of fear

You are the wings I never knew I had
The way out of feeling sad
The want of an everlasting moment
My answer to if true love is truly ever heaven sent

Glorious Allure

A heart as gentle as a soft summer breeze
With a caring soul that puts others at ease
Always so tender and sweet
That when you stand by her side it makes you feel so complete

To know her is all the reason to smile
Makes you happier than a bride walking down the aisle
For she is as precious as a child who never had a reason to cry
As glorious as the image of an angel in the sky

She is just such a delight
Makes every moment feel so easy and light
This very special soul born just for me
Who is everything that I want a woman, a lover, a friend and
      companion to be

Intertwined

You are the one
My very special someone
The one I am so very sure of
For whom I feel nothing but love

You are the one I want to reach for in the middle of the night
The one I want to see in the glow of the morning light
All I ever want throughout and at the end
The one in my life that I prayed for God to send

This is something I feel deep in my heart
A feeling from which I will never part
As you intertwined throughout all that I am and ever want to be
From within the captivating enchanting energy of you and me

With Love to You

On butterfly wings
In the melody of a song that an angel sings
Within the mystical energy of a full moon
In the comfort of a lazy hazy afternoon

In the laughter of children
The bliss of two hearts beating as one
To the depth of your soul
Within the peace of a spring morning stroll

Upon the air that you breathe in
In the happiness of feeling a new day begin
On this very special day
I send to you love in every way

Words

You whispered words into my ear
About how I had nothing to fear
How it was you that I could trust
That this was true love and not just a moment of lust

Such sweet words where you asked for my heart
Said that with it you would never part
How you and I were meant to be
For all of life and eternity

So precious was every word
Like listening to the beautiful singing of a songbird
As my inner child tried so hard to not hear the warning bells ring
From all of the others who said the same thing

Unlearning the Lesson

I had my heart broken
By someone with whom love was spoken
Whom I gave all of my soul to
From within a love I felt to be so true

This made me breakdown and cry
Made me feel like I wanted to die
As he just turned and walked away
Leaving me with so many words left to say

It all was just such a terrible lesson
In turning the happiness of love into the sadness of depression
Of which I now must somehow unlearn
If I am ever to hope that my spirit to go on will somehow return

Passing Moments

My world has sadly stopped cold dead
From so many thoughts that now run through my head
Which causes me to hurt so very much
From no longer being able to feel your touch

It is an emotional pain from deep within
That ends only long enough to once again begin
A pain not visible to the naked eye
Felt only by those that for a love had to cry

And as the moments pass the feeling does not go away
Leaving me to dread the coming of my each and every day
As I lose everything that I had become
To the pain of the loss of that to which I now succumb

Creation of a Star

People come and people go
This is how we learn and how we grow
For each teaches us what we should and should not do
Which direction for us is true

Over it all we exert what control we can
With acceptance of it all being a part of a bigger plan
Whereas we all do our part
In fulfilling the needs of the mind, body, soul and heart

This is what we embrace
As we create out of life our space within space
Where we ultimately become who we are
As unique to life as to the universe is a single star

I Butterfly

If I were a butterfly
I would never have reason to sigh
For I would be a Monarch butterfly with the colors of a rainbow
Illuminating with purple blue green orange and vibrant yellow

Where throughout my day I would fly from flower to flower
Bathing in the rays of a sun shower
As the wind blew gently against my wings
As I enjoyed the wonders of what life as a butterfly brings

There my life would preciously unfold
Unraveling from wondrous adventures untold
Where, as I rest my wings under the peaceful light of the moon
I would gave thanks to all especially to you for being my life-giving
    cocoon

Nearing the End

I have been around
Been lost and found
Felt a new day in the morning light
Fought my most horrifying demons in the darkness of the night

Laughed so hard with tears in my eyes
Cried so much from hearing so many goodbye's
Looked for inner peace in the quietness of a pew
Found myself in the magnificent wonders from a mountain view

I've truly been through a lot
With so many of which some I remember but none I forgot
And to tell you the truth you won't be my first for I have a past
But from the bottom of my heart and soul with love you will be my
    last

Gypsy Woman

I am utterly captivated by the soul of a gypsy
Entranced by all that shrouds her in a mesmerizing mystery
Can feel my entire existence howling like a wolf at the moonrise
As the magnificent image of her pierces the sight of my riveted eyes

The pure unbelievable feeling goes beyond love
Transcends everything I have ever been sure of
As her free-spirited soul dances wild in my heart
Ripping my entire emotional being and its control so willingly apart

It is all just so breathtaking
So wonderfully life-awakening
As my physical being screams in want to do what it was taught to
      forbid
Until I suddenly realized that my eternal soul already blissfully did

From Within

You are my everything
You make my soul soar
You are beyond a want and a need
I love you more and more

You are all I feel
You are all I think about
There is no me without us
With you I can no longer live without

You are my forever
Without you my soul will die
You take my breath away
Because of you tears of happiness are now all I cry

Without you I cannot breathe
This is a love like no other
You are such a blessing from above
Now I will never ever give my heart to another

Where I Always Want to Be

I move to a soft summer breeze
Taking each moment with ease
With no particular place to go
Allowing my heart and soul to just float with the flow

Such a feeling of tranquil peace
Filling my entire being piece-by-piece
As I feel so connected with all of life
With no noticeable difference between here and the afterlife

Just so calming this state of presence
Where everything makes so much sense
Right here where I always want to be
Inside the love of you and me

In the End

Fate has a funny way
Of surprising you day after day
One day it makes you question everything you are sure of
The very next brings you the deepest joy of love

No real rhythm or rhyme
Within no exact measurement of time
Just does and brings what it may
Without so much as even a word to say

But even if it brings you to the end of your rope
You should never give up hope
For at the end of this strife
It will bring the promise of the afterlife

Drizzle with a Little Sprinkle

It was rainy and cold
Causing the day to feel so dismal and old
With a blanket of clouds weighing so heavy in the sky
Causing the feeling of being in some long drawn-out sigh

Was just such a stillness to the air
Making everything feel so emotionally aware
Leaving me so captured between the feelings in my heart and the thoughts in my head
On this dreary gray day where I just wanted to hide in my bed

It all just felt like another one of those days
Where I was going to be left in some kind of uncontrollable haze
Until I felt your wonderful beautiful energy from behind my closed
     door
And then the weather just did not matter any more

Journey

Through the passages of this life
With influences of the unknown from the afterlife
We are on a joyful awakening we call a journey
From who we were to who we are to who we are meant to be

It is a process where we are being transformed
By the new that we must experience and by the old of which we are being re-informed
All of which is happening by the energy that created our eternal soul
That over us, if we allow, has utter and complete control

So just open yourself to all of the wonders of it
And let the joy of it all fill your heart, mind, body and the very depths of your spirit
As each new moment that we are in
Brings us closer to fulfilling why the journey had to begin

Lost

I am so lost without you
Find no worth in anything that I do
Everything just seems so meaningless and empty
Without you here to share it all with me

I actually find myself just aimlessly wandering around
Feeling like an unwanted item left in the "lost and found"
As I do everything I can to not lose my mind
From this terrible feeling of feeling so left behind

All so heavy that I just want to die
As all I can do is just shout and cry
As I feel it all starting to take its toll
As I feel that of it all I am losing control

Mannish Man

I am strong
Protector from all that is wrong
Provider for those I care for
With a determination that is felt to my core

I am dominant
At times overly adamant
Unwavering in my methodology
Ensuring everything is as it should be

I am rational
In control of all that is emotional
With tears held so deep inside
That are only seen by those in whom I confide

I am physical
With a physique that is functional
To withstand what is ahead
To satisfy in the want and need in the intimacy of bed

I am a man
Always fulfilling my part of the plan
Which of all I am so very proud of
Especially when I am a man to the woman I love

Making You Appear

My soulful screams for you are all I can hear
As my eyes begin to emotionally tear
Causing all of my feelings to feel so severe
Taking away all of the reason for any cheer

I am so empty when you are not here
Leaving everything so unclear
Giving me all the more reason to want you near
As I wish with all of my heart and soul that I could make you appear

This all is all so sincere
This feeling that is all so clear
That it is being without you that I fear
For being together in love with you is all that I hold dear

Rainy Day Girl

She loves the rain
The way it softy falls against her window pane
The way it makes her feel so deep inside
The way it makes her feel that she no longer needs to hide

The feeling brings such a calm over her heart
As each single drop refreshes her heavy heart
As she stands face to the sky
Letting it wash away all the tears she had to cry

It is actually such a sight to see
As she dances in it with joie de vivre and glee
As she twirls all of her cares away
In the downpour of a rainy day

Poetic Hugs

Expressing feelings from deep within my heart
Of love I shared and love that fell apart
Soulful feelings that I have felt to the core
Of which some imprisoned me and some made my soul soar

This I do with cause
Not just because
As meaningful as the stars that fill the night
As graceful as an eagle in flight

All expressed without reservation or fear
From behind a smile and sometimes from within a tear
Of which all I share with you
So you may not feel so all alone in all that this life puts us through

Precious Gift

I have so much to share
The tenderness of the way I care
The joy within my every touch
The depth of what I offer never being too much

It is in my nature for I am love
Created and blessed by the lord above
To bring bliss to the heart of the one I adore
To faithfully give my precious gifts forever more

This is my destiny the core of my soul
Which must be given and never stole
For what I have been blessed with is delicate and rare
Which when given to the one I love will never leave them in despair

Precious

She will not let people know
Would never let it show
She keeps it even from herself
High above on an emotional shelf

It is actually something that has been in her all along
That she has overlooked for so long
Something that she will not admit
Even if it would be to her benefit

What is good is that it will never go away
Will always be in her to stay
Forever and ever since before she could crawl
The fact that this precious woman is more special than all

Silk and Feathers

She struggles day in day out
To make sure they do not go without
Doing everything she can to make ends meet
To somehow put shoes on their feet

So astonishing this woman so determined and proud
Refusing to get lost within the crowd
Unwavering in making it on her own
Even when she sometimes feels a little afraid and so alone

Such a strength that comes from deep within her heart and soul
To never give up or lose control
As she faces each new need with an outward sense of calm
This brave woman that fends for her family as a single mom

So Far Away Yet So Close

She is so far over there
And I am so far over here
So far apart from one another
Each so much wanting to be with the other

It is all such a strong desire
That burns in us like a raging fire
Calling to our hearts and souls
Forcing us to always be on the edge of our self-control

But there is one consolation in all of this
That even though we cannot even share a kiss
That no matter how far apart
We are always so close in one another's heart

Tears

Some tears we cry are good
We would cry a million of them if we could
For they are from happy moments that come our way
Like when we laugh too hard at the funny things we say

Then there are the tears that are bad
That we cry because we are sad
Which we cry as a relief
Like when we suffer through the feeling of grief

Both we cry without control
As they force their way from the depth of our soul
To do as we need them to do
Make room in us for what more we must go through

Words of Love

You might ask me why
To her I am such an expressive kind of guy
Why I shower her with so many words of love
Why I always say to her that of her I cannot get enough of

I guess it is true
This is something that I certainly do
Express with all of my zeal
Every magnificent feeling that she causes me to feel

All I can say
That I am really not different in any way
For I am sure that you would too
If you felt the love that is felt between us two

Free to Soar

Deep within her
Are the imprints of the way our ancestors were
From a time less restrained
Where our souls did not feel so cautioned and chained

To see her is to actually gaze into the essence of love
Feel the proof of heaven above
Understand the space between space
Embrace hope for the whole human race

This is what sets her spirit free
To be the way she was meant to be
The source of her unadulterated desire
That sets her soul blazing like a wildfire

Just so untamed and delightfully wild
This woman who is as innocent as a child
This vison of all that once was before
That allows, if not for just a vicarious moment, our souls free to soar

Promises Promises

We promised never to part
That we would forever hold on tight to each other's heart
That we would always be understanding and kind
To one another's faults we would be compassionately blind

It was all within the promises we spoke
Of how we wanted to see each other from the moment we woke
With you as my husband and me as your wife
Forever protecting each other from all of life

But forever came too soon
As we couldn't even make it to the honeymoon
Where in the end
I was not even sure if you were ever even a friend

Emergent of Self

We celebrate we sigh
We laugh we cry
We learn what love is about
And then learn how to live without

All feelings that lead to who we are
That some songwriter plays on her guitar
That lets us know that we cannot hide
From all that we keep so deep inside

Such is life's way
That takes us from day-to-day
Of which we learn to accept and sometimes try to forget
As it all adds the substance to our ever-evolving silhouette

The Journey Within

We are on a journey
Through all that we do and do not see
Guided by our inner light
To that which for us is right

This is a journey that to each is our own
But one where we really do not travel alone
For along the way we happen upon kindred energy
Where together our light helps shine the way to our destiny

This opens our mind and frees our soul
Transforming us in whole
From what we were at the start
To that which has always been right in our heart

Waves of Joy

You I know
From long ago
Before there were trees
Before even the birds and the bees

Everything about you and us just seems all so familiar
Beyond all sense of it ever being unfamiliar
From the very first moment I could sense it in my soul
That our two souls were at once one beautiful wonderful whole

This caused such a peace
Waves of joy that just would not cease
As I could feel deep within
That we are now once again as we were before the original sin

The Warmth of Her

She is as wonderful as she can be
A pleasure for the eye to see
So much more special than me or you
The very best through and through

It is a blessing from deep within
This sweetness that's truer than a virgin's grin
For it is pure love that runs through all of her soul
That allows her to give her heart to all in whole

Such a rarity this delightful woman of joy
Who embraces those around her with enchanting feelings for all to
      enjoy
That brings to each a warmth that is shown in their smile
That gives reason for living to all the whole while

Precious You

Illuminate with love
Channel the light to below from above
Be what you want the world to be
Be the drop of water that makes a sea

Vibrate with care from deep within
Help others know where to begin
Be the source of everything right
For those who cannot see with their heart be their sight

Be the one the only one
That special one to someone
In all that you say and do
Be the you that so wonderfully makes you you

Unimaginable

From a million miles away
Your enchanting touch took my breath away
Like you were right by my side
Leaving me emotionally nowhere to hide

So amazing was your touch
That to feel it forever would never be too much
As I opened up to you my soul
As you gave to me the very essence of you in whole

The feeling left my entire being aglow
From an energy that I never thought I could ever know
Unleashing unimaginable waves of soulful ecstasy
From a feeling of true love between you and me

Transcending to Me

I started this journey long before my birth
Which has led me to this place called earth
Where I learn of that which is here
From all that I see, taste, smell, feel and hear

This I embrace
This necessary journey through the human race
Which helps to guide me
From who I was to who I am to who I am meant to be

All of which is so wonderfully enlightening to the depth of the real me within
Where the true journey to me did begin
As this experience of this me starts to joyfully end
As the essence of my soul, spirit and being begins to transcend

Growing Pains

Today I was pushed to the edge of my emotional sanity
By all of the things in life that had to be
So much that I just wanted to give up
Was truly so tired of being a grownup

Really not sure what really did it
That literally threw me into a raging fit
But I screamed and yelled and even worse
I broke down and could not even control the need to curse

The whole feeling went on for what seemed like forever
It all was like being in some kind of blinding blur
As all I could do was pray for help through this fiasco
As I so desperately held onto the edge with just my little baby toe

In Time of Need

This world sometimes gets the best of me
With all of the things that I so agonizingly see
From the billions of animals being abused, tortured and killed
To the day-to-day suffering that leaves so many broken and unfulfilled

Such a burden to bear
As an empath feeling so much that is just so unfair
As others are so unconsciously misled
While so many others just turn their head

It all just makes me want to cry
And scream out in despair to the sky
In hope that it all may somehow end
As I hang on to my sanity in the arms of my caring friend

Could See Forever

My whole world finally felt right
Forever was so clearly in sight
For I finally found an escape from my despair
Within a true love with a woman so precious and rare

I could really feel deep in my heart that she was truly it
A blessing that could help me to forget
Just to think of her put a smile on my face
To get the smallest glimpse of her took my feelings to a special place

All I could feel and want was her and no more
For she was the one that made my spirit soar
Giving me all the reasons to never again be sad
That are now only just memories of a happiness we once had

Facing the Day

There are good times and bad
Happy ones and sad
Times when we do nothing but defend
And times we wish would never end

And it seems like it is all not by our choice
Having so little to do with the words in our voice
Like it is all just not a matter of what our wants are
Or how little we go or how far

It all just keeps coming our way
As we face each and every day
No matter if we do it with a smile
Or with tears in our eyes the whole while

The Disguise

She looks so rough
Tries to act so tough
Gives all the evil eye
Make it looks like she wished they all would die

You can see it in her walk
Can hear it in her talk
Can feel it in her stare
Tries so hard to make sure all are fully aware

But it is all a thin disguise
To make sure that no one may realize
That behind it all she is just trying to hide
She just cannot add another tear to all the tears she has cried

So Silly

She is so silly
Just a big ole silly willy
From her silly hair to her silly toes
Her silliness just grows and grows

It is what makes her so much fun
Such a joy with no comparison
From all of the silly things that only she can do
All the silliness that makes everything feel so new

So infectious it makes you want her more and more
Makes you forget that there was even a moment before
And in the end there is only one thing to say
To be with her makes for a fun silly day

So Rare

So rare to find a best friend
That will hold you tight until the end
To stand by your side with a caring heart
Someone that you can feel love from even when you are so far apart

Such a feeling that it makes you strong
Which helps you through all that may be wrong
That makes you feel so thankful for
Making it all so different than before

And it is with joy that I must say
That I feel so blessed on this day
For no friendship is more special or true
Than the one that I share with you

In the Shadow of Her

She is as brave as she can be
Fights beyond the fear of what she cannot see
This woman so independent and strong
Who will not accept what she knows to be wrong

So determined in her ways
From her beliefs she never strays
Makes it all crystal clear so all may understand
That what must be is where she will make her stand

Such an inspiration to feel her soulful power
That comes from deep down inside of her
Where fears imaginary or not will ever stop her from being the woman she wants and needs to be
Which leaves me in awe as I stand in the shadow of all that she is and will ever be

Perfect Stranger

She's a woman of mystery
Wild, untamed and free
Strong both in life and spirit
Admits she's fragile, but you'll never hear it

So unpredictable this woman of impulse and instinct
In each and every way so remarkably distinct
Amazingly clever, truthful, funny and fun
Try to pin her down and as fast as she can, she'll run

And if she lets you gaze into her eyes you will gaze into her heart and soul
But of what you see she is in complete control
Where the more you think that you truly know her
The more she fascinates you by being such the perfect stranger

Nowhere to Go

The world goes on
As I sit here not knowing how to go on
In a feeling that leaves me lost and alone
With an emotional pain that hurts to the bone

Such a burden this misery is to bear
As my sadness fixates into a cold hard stare
As I ponder the course of my fate
From all the happiness I had to this moment of hate

All leaving me to question my next breath
As I pray for the arrival of my death
For when push came to shove
We stopped sharing such a precious love

Waiting

Sharing our self is so hard to embrace
So many lie right to our face
Draining the very essences of our soul
Breaking into pieces what once was whole

All just leaving us gasping for breath
Making us realize that there is something worse than death
Causing so much to question and doubt
As all we can do is cry and shout it all out

This makes it so very hard to trust anyone with our heart
To let someone into our deepest part
From all of the emotional pain that it puts us through
As we wait so hopefully for the presence in our life of someone
      precious and true

In Passing

There will be a moment
That I will pass without my consent
Where the reaper will not give me a choice
No matter what tone of my voice

And as I debate with him my fate
With examples of my love and explanations of my hate
I am sure he will have too many uncomfortable questions
That will for sure cause me to deeply reflect on all of my life's
    creations

Whereas when he gets to that question that I know he will ask for
    sure
About within this life do I think I could have had more
I will without a doubt look intently into my life
And with all of my heart and soul turn to him and say no
for I ended it all within the love of you as my wife

As Tears Fall

She is and has always been there
With such tender loving care
Ever since I was a child
Even more so for her beloved grandchild

So gentle, yet so very strong
Always making us feel that we belong
For when it all somehow spiraled out of control and fell apart
She was always such a strength of comfort and support from deep within her heart

But now life has caught up to her
Draining away from deep within the life energy light of her
Where now we just want to let her know
That throughout it all we with all of our hearts loved her so

A Beautiful Secret

There is an ancient secret I wish to share
With those for whom I truly care
Of which I have never told anyone before
That I will now share with everyone I adore

It is a secret that has been handed down
Passed on from crown to crown
To those of great trust
Of which now with it you can do as you feel you must

But with such knowledge comes great responsibility
To act wise with what you will now see
For it is a knowledge that you will never ever be able to forget
That under our clothes we are all so beautifully naked

Purple

I watched as you felt someone's emotional pain
And reached out to them with nothing in return to gain
Bringing a warmth to their heart
Right before they fell apart

This brought a tear to my eye
As I felt you both start to cry
From the depth of their release
That filled their heart with the feeling of peace

There, but not only there I realized how special you really are
How the light within you shines as bright as the midnight star
That just from your loving and caring embrace
You have the ability to take away the despair from someone's face

Unambiguous

I am strong
The maker of what for me is right from wrong
Guided by ways of old
To a destiny yet to unfold

I am victorious and magnificent by design
A goddess born from goddess's bloodline divine
Which brings a sense of peace and harmony
From deep within me with me

Of this all I am not scared
As I face my journey unequivocally prepared
For I am woman
And I have just begun

Between the Words

To each other we speak
Of which gives into each other's soul a small peek
To that which we want each other to see
To fill the mind with our intended imagery

This is how of ourselves we share
With words that flow through the air
So as to somehow convey
That which we try so hard to relay

Truly such a graceful dance
A delicate emotional romance
Where we each react not only to what we think we heard
But to the energy and love between each and every word

Stay

I don't want someone just for the night
Who will run out at the break of light
Leaving me with the sensations that I now crave so much
From everywhere they found a way to touch

This is not the kind of love I want to share
My need is for something much more rare
Where we give to each other forever more
That which we have given to no one else before

For it is here within this extraordinary moment
In an instance of an amazing soulful attachment
That the wonderful depth of fulfillment is known
From the heartfelt love that is so enduringly shown

Sacred Love

Love the way we loving play
The way we laugh at the things we say
How everything feels so right
Whenever we are within each other's sight

It is truly such a beautiful love
As delicate as the heartbeat of a dove
As special as a new day sunrise
That is all felt in the gaze into each other's eyes

It is what I will always live for
Of which I will never need of anything more
For you are and have always been
My eternal soul's twin

One Wonderful Day

Today was a perfect day
Paid all of the dues I had to pay
Danced wildly like no one was around
Reacted so happily to each and every sound

Reconnected with those I love
Even those who are now in heaven above
All caught up on that which was behind
Found everything that was once so hard to find

And throughout it all
I sometimes stumbled but did not fall
And as the day slowly slipped away
I wished for all the joy of such a perfect day

In the Silence of Me

Into myself I retreat
To make whole all that has become incomplete
As I replenish all that I have given away
To that of which was on my way

This is my sacred place
My space between space
Where I alone find harmony
With all which is a part of me

So powerful is this
That fills me with the energy of bliss
A state of Zen
So I may, with peace of heart, soul and mind, continue on my way
      once again

Falling

In you I trust
To let go of the things that I must
So I can be who I was meant to be
Within a love between you and me

Such a wonderful feeling to feel
How it helps all of the wounds to heal
As I let go into the joy of it all
As into the depths of you and us I so willingly fall

So glorious is this between us two
Of which makes each moment feel so brand new
Within the sacredness of this love
That feels as wonderful as being an angel in heaven above

In a Friend's Hand

I was walking with a friend
Who to me is a Godsend
Where we talked about things we saw
With peaceful moments where we didn't speak at all

It was all just so wonderful
How for the moment we were just so very thankful
As we walked hand-in-hand
Without so much as a need to understand

And with each moment being better than the one before
We wanted and needed for nothing more
As the joy of the moment felt like it would never end
As we both felt so safe from it all in the loving embrace of a friend

Deific Light

I saw what she could see
Which she saw deep inside of me
As she gazed into my essence
Enlightening the very depth of my existence

Could truly feel within it all the wisdom of the ancients
Causing me to fall to my knees in pure reverence
Where my entire being awoke to her insight
To the energy of her divine feminine light

It was all about her intuitiveness
Her innate instinctiveness
Within which I felt as free as an uncaged bird
As between us we spoke the depth of love without ever saying a word

Angel of Bliss

Such a kindness from deep within
A soul free of earthly sin
With a smile that lights up the darkest room
And a natural beauty that makes a man want to be her groom

Always there for those in need
No act of goodness too hard a deed
Eyes so deep that they lock you in the moment
An underestimation to say she is heaven sent

Such a blessing this woman of happiness
This angel of bliss
Who is a dear precious friend to each and every one
With a God-given inner light brighter than the morning sun

Caged

I cannot kill you
No matter what I do
You just keep right on living inside of me
Draining the life from all else that might be

No matter how hard I try
No matter how many tears I cry
The thoughts and feelings of us just linger
Distorting my vision of me into a shadowy blur

All such a battle within me that my emotions relentlessly wage
Making me feel like a tortured animal captured within a cage
Which one day I will break free of
As I slowly learn to let go of all that I have come to love

You Came

I really did not expect this
Was not looking for someone to kiss
Was really content with the thought of making it to the end
With at best finding someone to be a best friend

But then you came along
And showed me that I am really not that strong
To overcome what the soul may feel
Whenever a love is true for real

Now I expect no less
As I feel upon my heart your gentle caress
To spend my remaining days
Being everything I can to you in all ways

I Breathe

I breathe into your depth
Immaculate love with each and every breath
Unconditional and complete
So very tender and discreet

This I do without restraint
Above all earthly constraint
So it may fill the deepest parts within you
With a love so heartfelt and true

So breathe deep
That of which is always yours to keep
Every breath of love from which I will ever part
That I breathe only for the love felt within your heart

Surrender

Between us there are no secrets
No doubts or regrets
We tell each other everything
Do not hold back a thing

For everything about us feels so wonderfully connected
Willingly unprotected
With no worry of being vulnerable and exposed
From within the sense of feeling emotionally reposed

All in the name of love
Within the us that we are so sure of
With caring thoughts and feelings for the other
In the tender trust of one another

Touching

If I were with you
I would enjoy everything that you do
From the way you brush your hair
To how you just breathe in the air

If we were together right now
I would give you a vow
To never allow for one precious moment
To go by without making you feel heaven sent

If I were right now in your presence
The feeling would be just so intense
That we would not be able to withstand
Just the simple touch of each other's hand

Emergent Youth

Moving a bit more slow
Somewhat more hesitant about the things I don't know
Ache in places that I used to play
Hair just a little more gray

Memory just not as strong
Passing of time much too long
Just a little more on my own
At certain times can hear me groan

No doubt that I got old
Just a little less bold
But one thing from which I will never part
I will always be young at heart

In My Darkest Night

In my moments of loneliness you are there
In the middle of my despair I feel your care
Whenever I am lost it is you that I hold on to
When I am at the end of it all you show me what next to do

I truly find comfort in the magnificence of just seeing your face
The peace within it fills all of my empty space
It is like gazing into an eternity of bliss
Where I am wanting nothing more than to be a part of all of this

All just so very wonderful how you do this to me
How you find a way to always help all that is beautiful to be
Where I now hold on to you so very tight
To help me through my darkest night

Dissipating Haze

Been one of those days
Felt like I was doing everything from within a haze
With every moment leading to the next
Each leaving me that much more perplexed

Just seemed like there was nothing I could do
To stop everything that I was going through
With the feeling of it all being on the brink
Like it all was moving just one step out of sync

It all truly was just so emotionally hard
Where I could not for a moment let down my guard
Until I finally made it to the night
Where she once again made everything alright

A Song Unsung

Should I dare
Express the depth of a love I cannot share
For it might not change the way we are
Of all the things that have brought us this far

Should I not keep it buried deep within
And not let what might or might not begin
Should I not hold on with all of my might to the moments of now
For is not what we already have more important somehow

My only hope is that she will feel it in her heart
The pain I feel whenever we are apart
As a love so true goes unsung
As I retain each word of love on the tip of my tongue

Transcendent Love

In the heat of an amazing moment
We gave our consent
To know each other in a biblical sense
From deep within our precious innocence

There and only there
We gave all of which is sacred and rare
As the passion and desire burned deep within
With each magnificent ending being just another way of how to
      begin

Leaving us to see feel know the very sanctification of its magnificence
Engulfing consuming the very meaning of our existence
Beyond the simple pleasures of the physical
To that which is so transcendental

Sharing Thoughts

Been thinking a thought all day
How it started I just cannot say
Just came to me without control
Taking over my mind body heart and soul

Was just such a powerful thought
So many feelings that it brought
Truly made me wish that I was not alone
Even caused an unexpected moan

It all became just so intoxicating so utterly compelling
Pushing me to the edge of uncontrolled emotional yelling
From all of its pinned up rapturous passion
As it all lead to the wanting of sharing it with someone who was thinking the same one

Radiance

I give freely of me
With all that I am and will ever be
Unconditionally and from the heart
Leaving joy for everyone from whom I do and do not part

It is energy from deep down
To help alleviate the slightest frown
So that all may only feel at peace
From within a light that I release

So take of what I share
As the essence of me fills the air
For I am a child of light
Illuminating love as we stand in the darkness holding each other tight

Such Are Things

With so many things
Of which my day brings
I deal emotionally blind
By the thoughts of my rational mind

Then there are these other things
Of which my day brings
That I determine what is what
From the intuition of my gut

But then there are yet these other things
Of which my day so wonderfully brings
That just flows right from the start
As I feel through it all with the deep love of my heart

Such are the things
Of which my day brings
That I get through without the use of words from a scroll
With everything that is of my soul

Smiling Heart

She is a joyous one
Makes just gazing into her eyes so much fun
Truly a captivating sight to see
As the mere sight of her touches the depth of all that I will ever be

Just so wonderful to have her here
Right next to me making everything so clear
With all of her exquisiteness and allure
And an innocence that makes the most sinful feel pure

All so very incredible
Falling in love just so inevitable
Pushing the very essence of living to the extreme
As being with her is just like being in a dream

Fornication

Back in the day
When kings and queens had their way
They told us what to do
Like whom we could get married to

They even went as far as to limit our each and every word
Which was really so very absurd
How we could say poop but could not say shit
Even though each means the same when you use it

This all carried over time
Where the use of certain words can even be a crime
Even though most words really do not mean a thing
Like the word we made up from when we were under the rule of
"Fornication Under the Control of the King"

Seeing the Light

I was idling at a red light today
Waiting for it to change so I could go on my way
As thoughts ran through my head
About why wasn't I somewhere else at that moment instead

On this and so much more I started to ponder
As each thought started to wander
Taking me in and out
Of what life was really all about

It all started getting really deep
So much that I started to weep
As I finally started seeing everything that was once unseen
When suddenly the light turned green

Beyond the Morning Light

She called me baby all night long
Like she was singing the words from a love song
Causing my heart to dance and rejoice
As I could feel the essence of her love in the very breath of her voice

Made me feel so very special
With every moment being so amazingly exceptional
Filling the very soul of me with bliss
As I could feel the depth of her in her kiss

It was just such a beautiful night
That went on well beyond the morning light
Where to all of my desires she never said no
As she embraced me like she was never going to let me go

Beautifully One

We make love so wild and free
Each touch pure ecstasy
As our bodies so passionately talk to one another
So wonderfully bringing out the essence of the other

All taking us from somewhere
Between acting like wild animals with abandon care
To tender lovers
Gently taking away the need to hide our innocence beneath the
        covers

Just all so breathtaking
This magnificent instant of giving and taking
Of being in and out of control
Within this glorious merging into one beautiful soul

Lifting the Mask

As the sun sets
I ponder my regrets
So as to clear my mind
Of that which holds me behind

This helps me to sleep
And sometimes causes me to weep
As I so patiently deal
With all that I feel

By far this is not an easy task
To look behind the lifelong mask
To face the me that I need to see
So I may someday be the me I hope to be

The Wide Open Door

I saw the door to you was open wide
And could hear you calling from far inside
Which caught my attention and my eye
As I was so casually just roaming by

So I walked right in without making a sound
With intrigue to look around
As it was not my intent to impose
Just could not resist why just to me the door was not closed

It all felt so special as the first thing I saw
Were the precious pictures of you the child on the wall
This brought a smile to my heart
To see the you at your start

I then again heard you call
From somewhere down the hall
Where I marveled at the magnificence of your décor
As the hall opened into the depth of your soul's core

And as I ventured down the hall and from room to room
I felt the energy of you pulling me to your bedroom
All so powerful all so strong
That I just knew that this was right where I would always belong

And as the moments turned into days and then into years and years
It all became so very clear
That I had no longer a need to roam
For right here in you was where I finally felt at home

As I Woke to You

I woke in the middle of the night
Well before the morning light
To whispers of love from you
From the soulful connection of us two

It was such an easy awakening
Like waking to the sounds of spring
As your voice felt so beautifully gentle
Like feeling the breath of a holy angel

And as each word fell so softly into my heart
I could feel upon my lips a smile start
For within your voice I could hear the depth of love
As if I had woke in the light of heaven above

Impassioned Scream

You, in every way
Take my breath away
Make me so weak in the knees
Cause my soul to scream please please please

Just all so captivating
The feeling you are creating
That surrounds my entire existence
Which I wholeheartedly give into without resistance

For you truly take my breath away
As I embrace you in every way
As I fall to my knees
Screaming please please please

From Within the Light

As those goddesses before me
I will stand strong against all that should not be
To fight with all of my light
For that which my enlightened ancestors had to fight

This is what has been passed down and taught
That against all that is wrong the fight must be fought
So all that is right may persevere
For all that will one day be of here

This right I will defend
Until beyond my valiant end
Which of this promise I will not release
For I am a goddess warrior of light, love and peace

End of Ends

To everything in this life there is an end
That starts a beginning towards another end
Until we finally transcend
To a beginning that has no end

This is what takes us through life
To that of an afterlife
Where we come face-to-face
For the reason of all ends within this place

With it all just being a small part of a divine plan
From which all beginnings began
What makes up our eternal soul's heart
That began all ends right from the start

Hit and Run

Today I ran into someone
And did not even stop to see what I had done
The feeling weighed so heavy on my soul
The overwhelming emotions just so hard to control

It was not like I saw her
The whole moment was just a blur
She just caught me so unaware
As she just came out of nowhere

And even though I could hear how my four wheels squealed
She still bounced right off of my windshield
Which brought such a heart wrenching tear to my eye
For she was such a beautiful butterfly

Play Play Play

I play
To pass the day
As moments fade into the past
As I take very little too fast

It is in my nature
To just frolic within nature
To have fun
Just being in the sun

This is how I live my life
As if this was the afterlife
Enjoying the things that I do
With friends, family and especially you

Until You

I was born
From heaven was torn
Replaced my wings
With what this life brings

Was not really sure why
With here being a reason to cry
That this had to be
Instead of forever in eternity

Really such a burden to bear
Why I am here and not there
Which I felt had no reason to put myself through
Until I fell in love with you

Brave Volunteer

I was in heaven with wings on my back
In a room way in the back
With other angels playing around
About who could make the funniest sound

When from the front of the room in a distant voice
I heard Him say that the task was our choice
So I raised my hand to ask
What was the task

When all of a sudden
He said thank you for being the one
To be brave enough to volunteer
And that is how I ended up here

Feeling Words

Words are so powerful
Can make us feel so wonderful
Which lifts us up
As do words used during worship

But then, just like sticks and stones
That break your bones
When certain words are spoken
They leave us so emotionally broken

Of which none are more powerful in any way
Than the words the one we love does and does not say
For of all the words said
Their words have the most power to make us feel alive or wish we were dead

In Your Eyes

Through all of the long lonely thoughtful nights
To the cold harsh empty glow of the neon lights
For far too long I searched to find me
To find what really makes me happy

With each endeavor
Leaving the feeling of never
All just leading me astray
To experiencing one more thing that made me feel so far away

It all just left me feeling all so very weary
Leaving my eyes always feeling so very teary
Until much to my joyful surprise
I found what I was truly looking for in the depth of your loving eyes

Dreaming a Dream

I was sound asleep
So peacefully deep
Where dreams are kept
That I dreamed while I slept

There is where I saw
Images that left me in awe
That caused me to feel
As if everything there were so very real

It all was such a delight
With it all feeling all so right
As I could feel in the deepest parts of me
That my dreams were just as much me as my reality

Silent Hurt

When I get hurt I don't get mad
Even try hard to not stay sad
What I do in an instant
Is to get very distant

It is not to hurt back
Or to use it as some sort of attack
I just get so emotionally distraught
So lost in dumbstruck thought

For it is not just anyone
Who has such power to stun
It is only those whom I love who can hurt me
That leaves me in such speechless agony

Nowhere Fast

We run
To keep up with the sun
In a world that won't stop turning
With all of its earthly yearning

This we do day in day out
Without really knowing what it is all about
We just keep putting on our running shoes
Trying so hard to not be the one who will lose

But in the end we are just running in place
No matter how fast our pace
No matter how much we think we are proving
After all it is just the earth that is really moving

Before

Before the stars in the sky
Before the reasons to laugh or cry
Before the beginning of time
Even before there were words to rhyme

Before a beginning or an end
Before the need for a friend
Before there was prayer
Even before there was a need to breathe the air

Before the birds and the bees
Before the flowers and the trees
Before there was even the morning dew
There was my endless love for you

Omnipresence

Every time we part
It leaves emptiness in my heart
Always makes everything about me feel so wrong
No matter when or for how long

Just such an agony
Leaving me in such misery
As I know not what to do
When I am not the other half of us two

For my whole sense of pleasance
Depends solely on your presence
As it is at this very moment in time
That I am at one with all that is of and beyond this lifetime

To Hear You

Had a hard day
Had to listen to what so many had to say
Whether I wanted to or not
All tying my nerves into a knot

Just so many voices everywhere I went
All giving me their two cents
Was all just such an ear-full
With most of it turning out to be bull

But at the end of the day it all really did not matter
Could feel that it all was just chitter-chatter
As I lay in the arms of my sweetheart
Listening to the tender beat of her heart

Fading Away

Haven't seen you in a while
So miss your smile
I hope all is okay
Do know that you are always in my prayers when I pray

Not really sure why it is that we lost contact
Why to the loss we did not somehow react
Seems like we just let each other fade away
Just a little more each and every day

Really just so strange
How things change
Without so much as a real understanding of why
Even when we can feel in our hearts the urge to cry

Driven to Tears

We had our ups and downs
Our days of laughter and our moments of frowns
And throughout it all we embraced each other tight
Comforted each other until beyond it all once again felt alright

We stood strong side-by-side
From each other our true self we did not hide
And so closely listened to what the other had to say
For we just knew that it was our love that was lighting the way

We truly were in and had so much love
A feeling that we were both so absolutely sure of
Then within a breath of a moment you left without a trace
Now all that is left of it all is my tear stained face

Enraptured

You took my breath away
From a million miles away
As if you were right by my side
Leaving me emotionally with nowhere to hide

So amazing was your touch
Nothing about it seemed to be too much
As I opened up to you my soul
As you showered me with the essence of you in whole

To it all such a natural flow
With an energy that left us both in an euphoric glow
Unleashing unimaginable waves of soulful ecstasy
As it all formed into the oneness of you and me

Never Before

For us I smile and sometimes cry
Feel so alive and then at times feel like I could die
All touching the very depth of my soul
Which over it all I have no control

Of this all I give myself freely
For us embrace even the very loss of me
So as to be at one within all that I feel deep in my heart
From within a true love that I felt right from the start

Not sure why this all is so
Why I am so willing to just let all of me go
But one thing I know for sure
Is that you make me feel like I have never felt before

The Blessing

She is a soul so rare
Of the world she does so care
Not just for the happiness of one
But for the peace and salvation of each and everyone

And if you are really lucky
She will consider you a friend to be
For it is at that very moment
You would realize the she was really heaven sent

Back and forth and back and forth
Not just the first time nor the second but at least the fourth
About how special she really is to this place
About how she is really a blessing to the human race

Beyond the Stare

Like many I hide my pain
Try so hard to not show others how I am slowly going insane
Don't let them see behind my thinly veiled smile
Hide my shoes so they don't see the wear from me walking my dreaded mile

Always trying so hard to keep all at an emotional distance
Distract all with words like "for instance"
So they don't see what is really going on
How far gone I am really gone

Just all so hard to even feel hope
As all I can feel is the end of the rope
With it all being such a heavy burden to bear
Whereas I thank God so much that I have friends like you who can
    see
beyond my cold hard stare

Naked

I wear my feelings on my sleeve
Cry whenever someone has to leave
To all pour my heart completely and utterly out
Give all of everything I am to everyone I care about

To the emotional core of me there is a bottomless depth
The feeling of love is on my each and every breath
Really feel the meaning of what others have to say
As everything and everyone so profoundly touches me in every way

All such a blessing and a curse
To feel so affected by all of the universe
As I make my way through all that has to be
As the emotional naked me

From Within Love

I love you
I love you more
You are my everything
You make my soul soar

You are all I feel
You are all I think about
There is no me without us
With you I can no longer live without

You are my forever
Without you my soul will die
You take my breath away
Because of you tears of happiness are now all I cry

Without you I cannot breathe
This is a love like no other
You are such a blessing from above
Now I will never ever give my heart to another

Beautiful As You

I see the beauty of you
In all the things that you do
In the energy that radiates from deep within
In the joy of your simple grin

Can hear it in every word that you say
In the way that you so blissfully play
In the way you make so many feel when they look into your eyes
In the way you take care of anyone who cries

Feel the true depth of it in the way you open yourself to others
In the way you make everyone feel like sisters and brothers
And especially in the one very special thing that you do
How you make everything around you just as beautiful as you

Unbreakable Spirit

It was all part of the plan
I would forever be his woman and he my man
Where together forever we would hold each other so very tight
With all the strength and energy of our love's eternal light

Such a joy to hear these words of bliss
That we sealed with an ever-loving kiss
From within a vow that we made from the depth of our heart
Where we swore to each other that we would never part

And between us there were just so many wonderful words spoken
Of how it all would never ever be broken
Which in the end left me feeling like dying
From finding out that of it all he was only lying

But as much as this shattered my soul
Leaving me to cry endless tears without control
I now have a new plan
To show the world and myself that no one can break the spirit of this woman

We Fall

With some people we fall in like
To these people our feelings we share with belike
With some as close friends and others closer than kin
Who are with us through thick and thin

With others we fall in lust
In the hands of these people the care of our body we trust
Some for no longer than as the night falls into the past
Others for as long as the feeling will last

Then there is that special one with whom we fall in love
Of which to give the very essence of us unconditionally we are certain
    of
Who to our life are as necessary as to life are the moon and the sun
Of all the people in this world you to me are and forever will be that
    one

Respectful Awe

Of women I post
As a humble host
In celebration
Of such a magnificent creation

In every way I can
Beyond the simple urges of a man
Through images, words and songs
As part of overcoming all of the past wrongs

Not out of lust
Or because for some reason anyone thinks I must
It is just simply
In reverence and honor of the divine feminine energy

Parasol

I stood in a downpour of rain
To wash away the tears of my emotional pain
From a sadness and despair
That left me without even the strength to care

I just did not know what else to do
From all that I was going through
Just stood there getting soaking wet
Trying so hard to just forget

And as the rain poured down
And I could find no other way to ease my frown
I was ready to just give up on it all
Until He sent you to share your parasol

Versions of Me

So many versions of me
Every decision made and not made taking me to and from what
    could be
All just a matter of turning left when I should have gone right
Going home when I should have stayed the night

Seems all so easy as the moments fade into the past
As the actions become memories just as fast
To make such choices that seems to have no link
That quickly becomes my life within a blink

And as I look I see that my life could have gone in so many ways
Could have had so many different things from what now fill my days
Of which there is one thing that is for sure and true
That I am happy that each one made or not has led to this love that I
    now share with you

The Wanting

I want you so much
Longing for your touch
To once again taste your essence
To feel the heart soul embodiment of your presence

Burns through me like a raging wildfire
Goes beyond mere desire
From it all there is nowhere to hide
Causes my whole existence to tremble inside

True underestimation to say that it is you I crave
That to the feelings of it all I am now an emotional slave
Of which I so willing give all of myself to
Now that I have fallen in such want of you

Life

We live we die
We laugh we cry
We learn what love is about
And then learn how to live without

All feelings that become who we are
That some songwriter plays on her sad guitar
That lets us know that we cannot hide
From all that we keep so deep inside

Such is the way of life
That makes you happy and then cuts to the bone with its cold sharp
    knife
Which we enjoy and then learn to accept and try to forget
So we don't end it all from the feeling of regret

Vivacious Verve

We are pure energy
That we feel from each other more than see
Each pulsating with waves of emotion
Directly connected to that of the light of the moon and the tides of
    the ocean

This is the essence of all
That which is from before and after the fall
That within itself is a powerful force
Of which we all are a part of and channel from the source

This is what attracts and repels
Influences and compels
Of which we should all share
From within the energy of love and care

The Journey

We are on a journey
Through all that we do and do not see
Guided by our inner light
To that which for us is right

This is a journey that to each is their own
But one where we really do not travel alone
For along the way we happen upon kindred energy
Where together our light helps shine the way to our destiny

This opens our mind and frees our soul
Transforming us in whole
From what we were at the start
To that which has always been right in our heart

The Silence of Love

We are a lifetime apart
Connected only by the feelings within our heart
Where we try so hard to hold onto to the other
From within this deep love that we feel for one another

So agonizing this distance we must bear
Leaving us both on the edge of emotional despair
As the want burns deep within our soul
From the feeling that we are two halves of a whole

And as we each reach out from within our need
Past that from which we can never be freed
We reassure each other of feelings that we are both sure of
With silent words of everlasting love

In the Shadows

Life is truly wonderful with her in it
Something that she will never admit
For she is just way too shy
Gets so embarrassed from praise that she could die

And even though there is so much to adore
You will always be left with wanting more
For she always places herself in the shadow of less
Which always hides the true depth of her specialness

And for this there is really no reason to be
For the real her is such a joy to see
For she is the essence of all that should be
Everything the rest of us should ever want to be

Broken Heartbeat

Most of us have that one
Who makes us come emotionally undone
Shattering everything that we are about
Leaving us broken and full with so much blame and self-doubt

Where no matter how hard we try
We cannot stop that they rip our heart out and make us cry
As they move on and leave us and our feelings behind
With all that we had to linger in our heart, soul and mind

This is what keeps us up at night
Holds us in the darkness within the light
As the little child that is deep inside
Just wants to run off and hide

But suffer as we may
We grow just a little stronger by the day
Whereas we somehow pick ourselves up
And go through the motions of being a grownup

That Someone

I need somebody
Not just anybody
It has to be someone who for me wants to really care
Who is truly an answer to a prayer

Not just someone but someone who really understands me
Who truly sees all that I am and can ever be
Someone who is really not afraid to show me love
Not just with words but with feelings that they are truly sure of

So please just don't promise me the world
Or the joy of some imaginary dream-world
Just let me feel deep inside
That you are that someone who no matter what will forever truly be
      by my side

Our Little Angel

There is a purity about her love
An innocence in it that is found only in those above
Which makes her beam with a gorgeous light
As bright as a spirit on an angelic flight

It is from the precious essence of her that she holds so close and dear
Something she just won't give away for fun or out of fear
For she feels it is a treasure to her and a gift to the one that she will
        one day give it to
In return for a love that she feels is eternal and true

It is all such a blessing to us indeed
A wonderful presence within this world that we will always need
For it brings hope to all that is and will ever be
That there will forever be someone like her that we will be blessed to
        see

Ray of Sunshine

I've only known her for a little while
Only once have I seen her wonderful smile
But from all I can tell she is such a meek and humble one
Thinks all that she does just should be done

She is actually like a sunshine ray piercing through a big black cloud
As her tiny little voice rises above all so loud
About how she only wants what is best for another
As her life here makes it all such a better place for the other

But hates so much when anyone says she is special
Says she is no different from anyone, is just as normal as all
But would be the first to admit that she is relentlessly there to the end
As she embraces her dark side to those who would hurt a friend

And when you see how hard she really tries
It would bring tears to your joyful eyes
For this woman from so far away
That lights up everyone's dark dreary day

September

There was a brief moment in September
That I will always cherish and remember
For there in a moment of a moment
I realized what true happiness really meant

Not very sure if I was really seeking it
Or if from sadness I needed something to help forget
Just knew that all of a sudden it all was crystal clear
That what I felt I now held so very dear

Truly all such an amazing feeling that till now I had been blind
As I felt it all deep in my heart, soul and mind
Which all actually was such a wonderful surprise
As it all happened just because I gazed into her eyes

The Peace of One

She is a unique form of grace
Can see it in every detail of her face
Everything about her so precious and admired
The mere presence of her so overwhelmingly desired

For when her soul touches you it takes your breath away
Leaving you in awe of her in every way
As with everything she does being so very caring and kind
With the hearts of others always on her mind

And through it all she makes her way with dignity and style
With a natural ease to spread love with her smile
All from within an existence so pure and surreal
Where of herself she only gives so others may heal

Playful

She is such a joy
Her playfulness makes me feel like a little boy
From the way she sticks her tongue out
To the way she pretends to pout

It is not like she does not care
For her sense of responsibility is all so rare
It is just that she says that if it has to be done
Then why not all for the sake of having fun

So refreshing her sense of being who she is
How she really comes across as a whiz
This wonderful woman of mine
Who always makes life nothing less than divine

The Strength to Cry

He knows just what to say
How to get me to agree to do it all his way
With promises of how he is going to give me so much
How I will feel nothing but love from his caring touch

So very hard to stay strong when I hear him speak
Not really sure what it is but I start to feel so very weak
As he says that he is going to make all of my dreams come true
Like a big beautiful June wedding where we will both say "I do"

So much have I waited for something like this for so very long
For far too long had to be so emotionally strong
Which has left me feeling so empty and all so alone
Where every day I have to find the strength to face it all on my own

But as much as I want to believe that he is good and that this is love
There is just too much about him that I am not very sure of
As it all starts to feel and sound like what was before
That I promised myself that I would never ever again allow any more

So to him I will say goodbye
As I cry the tears that I have to cry
For I'd rather cry tears that I cause myself to shed
Then cry tears from once again being battered, beaten and left for
      dead

Waiting on a Friend

I am just sitting here waiting on a friend
A friend I would do everything for to beyond my end
For it is a friendship that is precious and true
Takes away all the feelings of blue

For it surrounds me with love and care
Makes me feel so safe and warm there
In the arms of her sweet company
That is only there for just her and me

It is such a wonderful feeling of love
Wrapped in the bliss from heaven above
So much that it takes my breath away
Leaving me with the feeling that within it I always want to stay

Hopefully Waiting

Sharing yourself is so hard to embrace
So many lie right to your face
Draining the very essences of your soul
Breaking into pieces what once was whole

All just leaving you gasping for breath
Making you realize that there is something worse than death
Causing so much to question and doubt
As all you can do is cry and shout it all out

This makes it so very hard to trust anyone with your heart
To let people into your deepest part
So as to save us from the emotional pain we must go through
As we hopefully wait for the presence in our life of someone as
      precious as you

A Million Tears (2)

Today was sad
Lost everything I thought I had
Made me cry a million tears
That feels like I will cry for years and years

Just really cannot understand
How he no longer wants to hold my hand
How he thought it was best to just throw us away
Without so much as a few words to say

Just all so devastating was it
Just wish it all I could forget
Just so lost without knowing how
To get beyond the way it has left me feeling right now

But right at the moment that it all seemed too heavy to bear
Right as I gave up even the want to breathe the air
I felt you give me a hug with all of your might
Reassuring me that all was going to be alright

A Million Tears (1)

Today was sad
Lost everything I thought I had
Made me cry a million tears
That feels like I will cry for years and years

Just really cannot understand
How he no longer wants to hold my hand
How he thought it was best to just throw us away
Without so much as a few words to say

Just all so devastating was it
Just wish it all I could forget
Just so lost without knowing how
To get beyond the way it has left me feeling right now

The Hero Within

Within we must find the might
Whenever there is so much darkness to fight
For wherever there is so much wrong
We must find the strength to be strong

It does not matter if we are a girl or a guy
We must overcome the fear of what might make us cry
For the strength to do what is best for all
Comes when we decide to stand courageous and tall

And in this moment we will be our own brave hero
The person we never thought we would know
That leads to who we really are
The person that now will go so far

The Here of Lost Love

The moment feels so long here
Feels like it will never end here
Such a burden to bear being here
No air to help breathe here

Such a danger to be here
Somehow must find a way out of here
Must move on far away from here
Not let here hold me in despair that is here

For it is just not good at all here
So heavy a burden on the heart and soul here
Dragging all to the bottom of here
Causing all to slowly die here

But do know there is life beyond here
A life that replaces the despair that is here
With others who really care about you being so sad here
With hugs from the heart as you slowly leave here

Stand

There is no gray
In what I say
It is all black and white
Wrong from right

We must no longer accept the atrocity
That millions of animals are forced into misery
Inhumanely treated as just food
Or to just satisfy some new fashion mood

This all I am very sure of
That all of creation has a right to be treated with care and love
Where I make my stand
So just maybe one more person (and another and another) might
      somehow understand

Alone

There is no me without you
You are in everything I do
Everywhere I go
In all that I ever want to know

So much that my soul aches when we are apart
Causing tears to fill my heart
From the mere sadness of the void you leave
To the dreadful heartbreaking feeling that causes me to grieve

All so terrible this feeling of dread
That fills my heart soul and head
From the unbearable feeling of feeling so all alone
Without the love that you have so passionately shown

Caring Arms Of

This world sometimes gets the best of me
With all of the things that I so agonizingly see
From the billions of animals being abused, tortured and killed
To the day-to-day suffering that is leaving so many broken and unfulfilled

Such a burden to bear
As an empath seeing so much that is just so unfair
While others are so unconsciously misled
As so many others just turn their head

It all just makes me want to cry
And scream out in despair to the sky
In hope that it all may somehow end
As I hang on to my sanity in the arms of my caring friend

Brown Sugar

She walks around smiling
On her tiny little island
Spreading joy to everyone she meets
From the poorest of poor to the elite of elites

Such a delight
This source of light
Who cares so much
For all who gets to feel her emotional touch

Truly a sight to behold
As precious as a ton of gold
For she is like no other woman that has ever been seen
This Goddess this Angel this Philippine Queen

Tiny Songbirds

So very special without end
Was so worried today about a friend
With all of her heart she tried to be there
To show them that there was someone with care

So much that you could hear in her words
Like hearing the cries of a thousand tiny songbirds
For she so much wanted them to be okay
To find peace in everything that she wanted to say

This is a woman whom I call my best friend
Whom I know will one day heavenly transcend
For she is such a wonderful angel indeed
Always caring for and loving those in need

Freefalling into Emptiness

Today I cried
Of a pain from which I could not hide
As I did yesterday
And every day before that day

As I have ever since we decided to part
For it has sadly left a hole in my heart
Where all of my emotions freefall into
As they grasp for just one happy feeling to hold on to

Which I know I must somehow overcome
For tomorrow and the next day and the next will so demandingly come
Even as I face each with the lingering feelings of what could have been
Of a love that ended before it ever had the chance to really begin

Inimitable Love

Had a love that I lost
Which I tried to hold onto at all cost
Then a love that was so toxic to my soul
Where each moment within it took its toll

And then there was a love that made me so sad
From it not being what I thought I had
Then another love that brought me so much joy
As if I were a child unwrapping a Christmas toy

Truly, had so much love in my life
Each in its way as unique as a purple loosestrife
But never has there been a love so true
As the love so naturally felt and shared by us two

Grateful Surrender

I feel you in my heart
Where the sensations of you start
Deep within its core
Where no one has ever been before

This titillates my mind
Causing me to leave all else behind
As it stirs thoughts of new
From all of the magnificent images of you

All manifesting deep within my soul
Leaving me to vibrate so out of control
To that of all which is now only of our frequency
To which I gratifyingly surrender the very depth of me

In the Light of a New Day

I suffered but no longer do
Not in the way that the suffering put me through
For what made me weak for so long
In the end only served to make me strong

This by no means means I am well
There is still so much that I do not have the strength to tell
Of which remains a part of my heart and soul
That I still must find the strength to control

It is a fact that I must face
That I do with determination and grace
As I courageously make my way
From the darkness of the past to the light of each and every new day

Shadow

I talk like I heard my mother talk
I walk like I saw my father walk
I think the way my family thinks
I drink the way my friend drinks

I do what I see others do
I learned from what the teachers said they knew
I act like those around me react
I am that of which I attract

I truly often ponder why I am whom I have become
Why it is I am from where I come from
As I look deep into the shadow of me
To really see beyond all that have influenced me to be

To This I Give

It is you that I love
This I am so very sure of
For it is a feeling that I cannot control
That engulfs my entire soul

Just all so arousing to my each and every sense
With every thought every feeling of you so amazingly intense
Causing me to vibrate to my very core
As all I can hear is me screaming more more more

To this I give over my total existence
Entirely in whole without resistance
Now and throughout the ever of eternity
From within all that is and will ever be

I Want

I want to kiss your lips
Run my hands along your hips
Taste that of which is only you
Feel the sensations caused by all that you do

I want to hold you tight
Lay peacefully in your arms throughout the night
Gaze deep into your eyes
Wake to you with each new sunrise

I want to touch where no one has before
Hear you moan to feel for more
Fade away into the wanting way you say yes
I just want you nothing more and nothing less

Blessed Be

Witch of black
Who sometimes casts spells that attack
Not because she truly wants to
But most likely it is what was due

Witch of white
Who casts spells from within the energy of light
Where what she sends out it is told
She gets back threefold

Witch of grey
Balanced in every way
Her intentions are just
But she will cast as she must

Each so magical and pure
Enchanting with such sweet allure
Neither bound by tradition nor decree
Blessed in the ways of old are these witches three

Illuminating Care

Can you see it there
Over there
And there
Everywhere

It is just such a wonderful sight to see
Is in everything that is and should be
Illuminating all within and without
Eliminating any reason for doubt

For it is so amazingly bright
Brighter than any other light
Bringing joyful life to the very breath of air
This light of love from all that care

Essence of Love

I have thoughts in my head
About you and me in bed
Holding each other tight
All through the night

I have feelings in my heart
Of us never being able to part
As we move together from day-to-day
With only words of love to say

I have knowledge in my soul
How we make each other feel whole
That has been since the beginning of time
From within a love that transcends a lifetime

Introspective Love

With my three eyes I see a lot
Since before I was a wee bitty tot
Of all of what has to be
All of what I must see

Each having its lasting affect
Causing so much reflective introspect
As I embrace each and every feeling and thought
Of something that has to be taught

This all I take in stride
To a universal energy by which I must abide
That all rushes through me without control
Like when I see you that causes my heart to melt into one with my soul

Seeing Me

I decide
From what I feel inside
What about me is good or bad
What makes me happy or sad

This makes me me
The one I think I want to see
With all of my virtues and flaws
That I sometimes say it is all just because

Within this I try to see me at my best
As the master upon my fated quest
Where to see the truth of me and the disguise
I look at the me I see in the depth of your beautiful eyes

Within Love's Sleep

I woke from my sleep
Where the dreams of you I keep
The first feeling was of you in my arms
And how there we each felt safe from all of life's harms

Softly I pulled you close
Could feel you feel being within love's engross
With it all as soothing as a child's berceuse
As I shallowed my breathing as not to wake you from your peace

There, within this blessed moment, I felt you sink into my embrace
As a smile gently came over your face
Where, from deep in my heart, I started to happily weep
As I felt you fall deeper into your peaceful sleep

Running to You

In my past
I ran through life so fast
In and out of everything that came
Sometimes not even stopping long enough to catch a name

It wasn't that I did not care
Or in any way was trying to be unfair
I was just following my heart
Which lead me from each ending to each new start

I truly did not think I would ever slow down
As I made my way from town to town
Until now, where all that I was running to and from
Has ended right here at what we have become

Embracing Each Other

It's ladies' night out
Where you can hear them all scream and shout
Like lionesses out on the prowl
Having fun the way woman only know how

And the men are all out hanging with the boys
Playing with their big boy toys
Making noise with a hoot and holler
Acting as men do to their very last dollar

All having their own kind of fun
From the rise of the moon to the rise of the sun
While you and I have the most fun of all
Passionately embraced within each other's enthrall

Fanning the Flames

Lust alone has no substance
Especially when felt for someone just once
With its only true aim
To extinguish the burning of lust's red hot flame

This leaves much to desire
Running from fire to fire
Which in its self
Is only meant to satisfy oneself

This in the end rips your emotions apart
Weighing so heavy on your heart
For it has so little to do with seeking a truelove
And the real heat from fanning the flames of love

Morning After Beautiful

Last night
Everything was just so right
As we touched each other in every way
With our heart soul mind body and every word we tried to say

So wonderful and beautiful was it all
Entangled between control and an emotional free-for-all
Where with nothing left to assume
We became as close together as a bride and groom

Such was the night so full of pleasure and laughter
Felt deep into the morning after
For as we wiped the sleep from our eyes
We saw the love of us within each other's eyes

Sweet Caress

My life as the me I want to be has began
All is right of the wrong that once was done
No longer feel trapped within what I could not change
Brand new outlook on that which once looked so strange

Truly such a feeling that has no true compare
All as refreshing as a breath of fresh air
Where I am so fully engulfed within the energy of the original source
From within a verve so perfectly aligned with the universal force

Just all so wonderful to feel this way
How much I now look forward to each and every new day
For at last I feel the happiness of love's caress
All because you said yes

Nothing Came

Waited so long
Had to be so strong
Searched so deep
Trying so hard not to weep

Moments passing into hours, hours into days
Surviving in some uncontrollable blurry haze
Started feeling it was me to blame
As nothing ever came

Felt just so all alone
Emotional pain felt to the bone
Just did not know what else to do
Until I was breathlessly blessed with the presence of you

God and Goddess

She could feel my desire burn
My nervous excitement yearn
As I throbbed from deep within
To my intense lust to which I was giving in

And as I stood before her on the edge of all I could not withstand
She reached out and took me by the hand
And with such tenderness and grace
Led me to her sacred space

There my soul trembled and shook
As we both so willingly gave and took
Where like a god and a goddess
We together created euphoric bliss

Scars

People come people go
Some we wish would stay some we wish we didn't know
Each cutting deep into us from what they do
As they each touch us with what they put us through

This in part makes us who we are
The owners of each and every emotional scar
Of which some are only skin deep
While others are ones that we will forever keep

From this you need not hide
With me you can show them all with pride
For within each scar it is the depth of you that I see
Which makes them each so beautiful to me

Wholeheartedly Yours

Take me
My mind heart soul and body
And do as you may
As to your every wish I will obey

This to you I give
For as long as I live
Without condition
In complete submission

Of which I do so not out of weakness or because I must
But because I so unreservedly trust
That never in a millions years
Would you ever cause me to cry sad tears

All of a Sudden

My life has been so deranged
Everyday everything was always so rearranged
With so many ups and downs
So little laughter and so many frowns

Just all sorts of emotional drain
Burden to just remain sane
Lost to the meaning of why
Found by the meaning to die

Moment by moment the days came and went
Each doing so without my consent
But then all of a sudden there came you
And now what does it all matter now that I share a love so true

Sands of Time

The seconds go tic-toc
On the man-made clock
Telling us when to sleep, when to wake
Leading to the next candle on our birthday cake

The why to this I do not understand
How the minutes of big hand leads to the hours of the little hand
Not even really sure what it is good for
How we need it now but did without it once before

Really strange this counting of time
How it takes us from the past to the present to some future expressed in a nursery rhyme
And how it waits for no one
And flies by when we are having fun

Not really sure how all of this makes me feel
How they even say that time has the power to heal
But for sure there is one benefit in all that time puts us through
That I will spend an eternity of it with you

Silent Love

Today I smiled at someone
They smiled back from what I had done
Then I saw that one
Do the same to some other one

I then gave someone a hug
So they could feel safe and snug
From which their whole sense of being shifted
As the weight of the world was lifted

And then with all of my might
To everyone in sight
I shared love with all of my heart
Where we all silently vowed from this feeling to never part

As I Made My Wish

In celebration of my birth
Onto this earth
They placed the candles upon their holder
To show that I grew another year older

This made this day more special than all of the other days
In so many special little ways
From the joy heard in the birthday song
To the love felt in the wishes that my life be wonderful and long

And when it came time to make my wish
I blew out the candles with a heartfelt whish
Knowing all along that my wish had already come true
That I got to celebrate this day within the love of you

Angelic Warrior

We are angels heaven sent
Here to this one short-lived moment
To do what we can and what we must
In the earthly battle against all that is unjust

From this we do not stray
For in our hearts we know the way
As we forge a very clear path
Toward all of which does not lead to wrath

This we do from within all that is right
With the energy of love and light
Where at the very moment that we shed our mortal skin
Another beautiful heaven sent angel is sent to continue
what we were sent to begin

Awakened to Us

We woke
Between us not a word was spoke
As we could feel the energy of "want" in the room
Of that reserved to a bride and groom

Tightly we began to caress
With feverish passion began to undress
As we kissed touched gave and took
As the very essence of our souls vibrated and shook

So powerful so intense
So vehemently gratifying to every sense
As we pleased that of which was felt so deep
Where in each other's arms we so caringly fell back to sleep

Light of Love

All of what I write
Is of love and light
That rushes from deep within
From a feeling that prevailed long before sin

It is an ancient blissful energy
That is the heart and soul of me
That was placed in me since before the time of my birth
Which channels through the vastness of the universe and the dirt of the earth

This is why I am here
To fashion that which all may endear
So we may somehow remember when we were in heaven above
As we all embrace each other within this manifestation of love

Wish

We all have our want and need
Where for it we wish and plead
All part of us making our way
That helps us get from day-to-day

There's very little we can do to change this
For it all is what we think will bring us bliss
Of which is rooted in feelings deep down
The difference between what brings a smile or a frown

This is how we each fulfill our burning desire
By the things that we acquire
Where if I had only one wish that would come true
To fulfill my need I would give that wish to you

Between There and Here

You are always here
I embrace you here
I love you here
I want you here

I am always there
Love feeling you feel me there
Will always be there
There is where I belong and only there

Such a distance between here and there
Narrowed by the intense presence of what we share
For even though we are not physically one-on-one
Between there and here we are one

The You to Me

You are the run to my crawl
The stand to my fall
The soft to my hard
The healed to my marred

You are the more to my less
The sure to my guess
The feminine to my masculine
The pure to my sin

You are the strength to my weakness
The hopefulness to my bleakness
The light to my heavy
And most of all—you are the you to me

As You Give

You fill my heart
Pull me together when I fall apart
Show me the way when I feel lost
Always there for me at any cost

You make me feel brave when I am afraid
Come running whenever I need aid
Listen so much when I have so little to say
Help me to see eternity when I don't even want to face a day

You truly free my soul
Give focus when I am out of control
Reach the real me when I don't even know myself
Comfort my entire being when I really don't want to be by myself

So much are you a cherished presence in my life
The one I am so proud to call my wife
As you give to me a love so true
Where I really do not know how to live without the love of you

Lifetime After Never

I have such a feeling deep inside of me
That goes well beyond bliss and ecstasy
It is a feeling that rushes throughout my mind body heart and soul
Engulfing all of me in whole

Such a joy to feel what it does
Leaves the very depth of me all abuzz
As the strength of it leaves me gasping for air
As I embrace this true love that we now share

And with all that I feel inside
As you stand so lovingly by my side
It will be a lifetime after never
That I would ever stop loving you forever

Glimpse

I glimpsed a woman so fair
For one brief moment caught an image so rare
So magnificent that it brought peace to my soul
Made my entire being feel so completely whole

It was not a long one
Just long enough for my heart to come undone
Long enough to get the best of me
To send my feelings spinning in uncontrolled emotional ecstasy

For within this one magnificent beautiful moment
I gazed into a vision that was heaven sent
Which to all of my senses was such a delight
So much that I now need forever to have her grace my sight

Dare to Love

There is a love that we two adoringly share
Which is so full of tenderness and care
A love so special and rare
That to not give it to each other we would never dare

It is the kind of love that goes with us everywhere
That is no less important than the life-giving air
That to it there is nothing to compare
The answer to each and every prayer

It is a love that each day to the world we so intensely declare
As we commit to each other as into each other's eyes we so
        passionately stare
For in the end we are fully aware
That there is no better place to be than within the love that we share

A Love So True

I fell in love
With such a wonderful woman that I cannot get enough of
To whom I give all of my heart
Of which from her I will never part

It is a love so true
Embedded in everything I am and do
That fills my soul with happiness and bliss
Well beyond the joy of a very first kiss

So much that the passion of it all burns so deep
To the core of me where the precious treasures of my life I keep
Which gives meaning to my entire life
As I spend each moment of a moment embracing and cherishing her
      as my eternal wife

As One

You are always on my mind
Without you it is me that I cannot find
You are so deep in my soul
That it makes me feel so complete and whole

Just the thought of you takes my breath away
Allows all of my worries to just slip away
Just all such a joy to know you are mine
To feel that this all is by a God-given design

Which brings a smile to my heart
To know that I am in your heart
As I feel in this moment that our eternity has begun
So soulfully engulfed within our love as one

Emptiness

Been so long since we spoke
That everything about me feels so broke
Can't think can't even talk
Even feels like I am going to fall whenever I try to walk

Really feels so uncontrollably strange
Like I am on purpose standing downrange
Where I am just waiting for a bullet to end it all
As I cannot even find the energy to crawl

It is such an emptiness of thought within my head
With everything about me feeling so dead
Now that I had just a small glimpse of my life without you
Where I found no reason to any longer see life through

Breathtaking

I gazed upon a vision today
Was in complete awe without words to say
For I was stunned by what I never knew
A beauty so vivid and so very true

It actually caught me by surprise
At first I could not believe my eyes
How could something so breathtaking be
Without it ever before being there for me to see

So I blinked my eyes twice
Just to make sure that I was just not being nice
But truth be told
She is in fact a pure vision to behold

So Very Big

I was blessed with a big one
That brings satisfying joy to all when all is said and done
Of which I love sharing with all
To offset those with one that is too small

Just nothing like feeling others feel the energy of it throb
As it is as powerful as the will of an angry mob
Which is something that I try so hard to be modest about
But do love when it makes others want to happily scream and shout

This all is not just a myth
As attested by those of whom I have shared it with
That leaves them all with a smile even if we have to part
From the fulfillment of feeling every inch of my great big beautiful
    caring heart

Edge of Frenzy

My body trembles when I feel your love
Never quite sure if it is something I can ever stay in control of
Always hope that I will make it through the emotional frenzy
That I somehow won't be overwhelmed by the onslaught of arousing
    ecstasy

It is a rush that runs from head to toe
That makes me feel things that I never thought I would know
Burning through every bit of me like a raging fire
As I try so hard to not be embarrassed by my demanding desire

It is so intense that I sometimes feel like I am going to lose my mind
As I become to all else so helplessly blind
From the feelings for you that have taken over my heart and soul
That now leaves me somewhere on the edge of my self-control

Falling Away from Me

Every moment away from her is so agonizingly long
Causing the feeling to cry to be so painfully strong
It is like ripping my heart out one tiny piece at a time
Giving to my soul a sense of having no reason, rhythm or rhyme

Terrible feeling this feeling of being so lost
That takes its toll with so much cost
For it is to her I am bound
For within her my happiness is to be found

The truth is that it is unbearable without her by my side
A feeling that always leaves me so empty inside
For forever will it ever be
That without her there is no me

Freely Yours

So much do I want to be with you
And let you do with me all of what you want to do
As I lay before you with an open wanting soul
Of which I freely let you take complete control

This I will forever live and die for
A pleasure that all of me will ever want forever more
For it is within all of what you make me feel
That I find all the joy that makes my dreams all so real

To this I will always give
All of me for as long as I shall live
As I may always be a part
Of that special place within your heart

Glory of Love

It takes away all of my self-will
Causes my heart to stand still
Makes me feel the depth of me
Opens my eyes to all that I could never see

Brings so much joy to my soul
Releases my need for any self-control
Lights up my life in so many ways
To the joy of it my heart so willingly obeys

It is all so intense
To feel the glory of its magnificence
That makes me so proud to be in a love so true
Even prouder that it is a love shared with you

Glow

I saw the sparkle in her eye
Felt the excitement in her love cry
As she felt of her joy
From being so in love with this boy

I could tell she felt it all
That her feelings were in complete awe
As she spoke the words of love
Of something she just knew came from the heavens above

And in her heart I could feel she knew
That this one was the one that was true
As her feelings gave her an angelic glow
As I felt the love between us grow

Calling Her Names

Without hesitation or shame
I am always calling her names
Don't really care who hears me or what they may say
It is something I will always do each and every day

For it is with each that I do so from the heart
Especially when I use names like honey and sweetheart
And even more so when I call her love
And then even more when I call her an angel from above

And I really don't care how it may seem
When I call her names like a heaven sent and wonderful dream
Or when I say things like she is such a queen
For they are all true especially when I call her beautiful and pristine

But as true of her as all of these names may be
How each truly expresses what she really is to me
There is no better name—even more than when I call her divine
Than when I call her forever mine

Blessings

I love a woman so fair
With whom a deep love I intensely share
That makes life worth living
From all of what she is giving

This touches me so deep
And causes feelings that I will now forever keep
As the joy of her makes me whole
Bringing such a bright light to the darkest parts of my soul

And the best part of it all
Is not that of her I am in complete awe
It is how each day we are together
She brings to my heart the blessing of feeling so happy within her
    love forever

In the Sorrow of Nothingness

Spent the whole day buried within my sorrow
Questioning if I would even make it to tomorrow
As the pain ripped my soul apart
From the sadness felt so deep in my heart

Was such a terrible agony to endure
Leaving me empty and of everything so unsure
As I just sat in my nothingness and tried so hard not to cry
As I fought the feelings that made me want to die

And as the moments slowly fell into the past
I realized that this torment was going to forever last
As I tried to do the hardest thing I ever had to do
To live this life without the presence and love of you

One Moment Too Long

If I knew tomorrow came without being with you
I would not know what to do
For every moment of today would weigh so heavy on my heart
As with each breath I took I would feel my life slowly falling apart

And as I struggled with tears in my eyes
To somehow not be overwhelmed by the awfulness of what my soul did not want to realize
I would sink deep into the darkness of my dread
Wishing by the end of today I would be dead

This all I cannot bear to feel
For the pain within would never heal
For to not be together forever would be so wrong
Making living one moment beyond today much too long

Longing

I want you so bad
More than anything I ever had
Causing my soul to ache so much
For the emotional release from your passionate touch

All making me so weak in the knees
From the thought of you doing all that you please
As I succumb to all of my desire
As it all consumes my self-control like everything in the path of a
        raging fire

So breathtaking is it all
Leaving me not even the strength to crawl
As I reach out for all that you do
So I can release all of my love into you

Out of the Blue

I wanted to write you a love poem
So I allowed my mind, heart and soul to roam
To feel all of what loving you takes me through
So I could express all of my love for you

The first thought that came to mind
Was how such a beautiful wonderful companion as you is so hard to find
And how lucky I am of all
To share such a love that leaves me in complete awe

So my pen started to write
Of every word that felt just right
When all of a sudden from out of the blue
I realized that years have passed and I am still writing love poems to you

Immersed

We made love last night
Touched each other everywhere that felt so right
Satisfying each other's each and every need
Giving more and more to the moans of each and every passionate plead

It was all like being immersed in pure ecstasy
The way she gave all of her and let me give all of me
With each touch another want to enjoy
Each emotional release that much more of a joy

All leaving feelings that run so deep
Leaving so many memories for her and me to keep
As we held each other so very tight
As it all became another cherished part of our love's light

Enchanting

I see her in all of my dreams
Hear her in all of my satisfying screams
She is in everything I feel
Everything I pray for when I kneel

She is all I want and need
The reason to no longer plead
My forever and ever
The relief from the emptiness of never

She is my happily ever after
The joy in my laughter
For it is true that everything beyond her is just a blur
For I am completely and utterly engulfed within the captivating love
    of her

Heaven Above

I am so in love with her
If I were a cat I would have the loudest purr
Not because of her beauty and charm
But because of a feeling that her love truly means me no harm

It is just such a safe feeling there
In the embrace of her loving care
So full of everything she wants for me
All the joy that she wants to be

It is like a dream that will never end
Like having a heart that never needed to mend
All wrapped up in this feeling of love
From a woman sent to me from above

Darkness

I mourn for you every day
Miss you so much in every way
My heart feels so distressed and empty
Darkness throughout my entire being is all I can see

Sadness taking its course and settling in
The misery felt from so deep within
My soul so heavy no longer able to fly
Such a burden that all I can do is just sit and cry

Was really having the best time of my life
When I felt you as my wife
Now I have no life at all
Since the moment we decided to no longer call

Enchanted Room

In the middle of the night
When darkness puts out the light
I lay with the thoughts of you in my head
With such strong feelings of you circling my bed

So powerful is your presence there
That it replaces my need for air
As the energy of it all touches me in whole
As I can feel the spirit of you sink deeply into my soul

And as my heart soul mind and body uncontrollably reaches out
I find it all so difficult to not let out a shout
That I am right where I want to be
Engulfed within the enchanting love of you and me

Emotional Touch

Every waking moment I think of her
Every dream is all about her
She has become so much a part of me
That all else has ceased to be

It did not take much
All started from just one small emotional touch
And it did not even take long
For it is a soulful feeling that was there all along

But now that it is I will never turn away
Will give to her my endless love more and more each and every day
For there is one thing I know without doubt
That she is what my existence can now no longer go on without

As One Soul

For a moment we were not one
Everything we were so quickly came undone
My life sadly came to an end
Had no more reason to ascend

Every moment apart made me cry
Every tear made me want that much more to die
So terrible this feeling of grief
From the pain just no mercy of relief

But now we are together once more
With all of the love we felt before
With a vow to never again let it go away
To always be as one to our dying day

Forever

There is a time between now and the end
Where I will be with her as more than a friend
Where she will call me husband and I her wife
Where we will share our love for each other for the rest of our life

It will be a moment of celebration and bliss
Entangled with emotions that will be sealed with a tender loving kiss
As we take each other into our waiting and wanting souls
To fulfill that need to feel whole

And there we will stay
As eternity melts into a day
To live happily ever after
Within our energy of peace love happiness and laughter

Love, Laugh and Play

With each breath I take
While asleep or awake
I think and feel only about you and me
In our life by the sea

Where we will walk barefooted in the sand
Within the caring grasp of each other's hand
Gazing into each sunset and sunrise
That will rise and fall in each other's eyes

And there we will share
All the feelings of a love so rare
While we love, laugh and play
As the moments of our life together fade into the wonders of each
      passing day

Love Eternal

I am blessed
By her I am so tightly caressed
Within a love that is so hard to believe
From a feeling so hard to conceive

It is an experience that leaves me in total awe
From a feeling of love eternal
A love so precious that I am not even sure I am deserving of
A love I am sure came from above

Such a joy being a part of this
In the feeling of total bliss
From a love so rare
That she and I now everlastingly share

Hugs and Kisses

The sun rises and sets in your eyes
In the reward for living you are my prize
For you are the most wonderful part of my life
All that I ever want in a wife

Angels sing to me when I hear your voice
You are why each day I find reason to rejoice
For you are the best that I could have ever imagined for me
All that I ever want to be

Truly heaven is the angelic sight of you
The strength in all that I ever want to be and do
For you are the cause of our love-filled bliss
The one that I will forever more want to feel the love of my hug and
    kiss

No Wishes

I am so blessed
By her love I am so tightly caressed
So tight that it makes me cry
Tears of happiness from a love that I cannot deny

Such a wonderful feeling to be there
So engulfed by the warmth of her loving care
As she gives me all of her soul
All that she is in whole

It is all such a rush
So intense that I embarrassing blush
From this extreme pleasure of being whom she cares for
That makes me wish and need for nothing more

I Promise

I promise that my eyes will always only look your way
That our words of commitment to each other I will always obey
That for us I will always be strong
That toward you I will never do wrong

I promise that from you I will never part
That you will always have all of my heart
That my need will forever be for you
That my love for you will always be deep and true

I promise that I will always hold you tight
That I will never leave the loving gaze of your sight
That my kisses will always be full of love
And that my eternal life with you is what I will always and forever be
      sure of

In My Whispers

A whisper of love in the night
As I hold her in my arms so tight
Telling her everything I feel
About how much I believe that this love is for real

So soft and gentle the words do flow
Of how I will never let her go
All spoken from the depth of my soul
From the essence of me about how I am hers in whole

And as my lips gently part
To let my feelings flow from my heart
To form as words in the air
I whisper to her in her sleep the words of a love so rare

Captivating Magic

I wish she was here
Or that I was there
For when we are together
Our hearts are as light as a feather

It is a feeling that is so passionate and true
Making each day feel so brand new
Giving us both reasons to enjoy living
From all of the love we both are giving

It is not that we are not happy when we are apart
For we still have the feeling of being in each other's hearts
It is just that when we together fill a space
It all becomes such a captivating magical place

Ropes of Steel

Now that I have given to you all that I have to give
I no longer have control over how it is that I live
Over the peace of my heart and soul
Over the mind that I once had control

It is like I go about my life in a haze
In a complete uncontrollable daze
Reeling from the feelings inside
Blind even though I am so open-eyed

All from what I so deeply feel
That has hold of me like ropes of steel
That I cannot and do not want to break free of
From this feeling of sharing with you this intense overpowering love

Forever Us

You came into my life
And vowed to be my wife
It sent shivers of joy up and down my spine
How such a beautiful wonderful woman was now all mine

The elation quickly overcame my mind body and soul
Giving me the sense that I was now made whole
As the understanding grew moment by moment
That you and this love were heaven sent

And as we make our plans to be together now and always
To love each other forever in each and all ways
We endeared a promise to never ever let this end
That on each other we will always be able to depend

Depth of Love

I love her so
More than she will ever know
For it is so hard to find the right word
For such a word I have not heard

I tried using the word bliss
But the true depth of what I feel for her this word does miss
I even tried the word delight
But even that did not have enough might

For to explain what I feel
Does not compare to anything real
And it is safe to say that this word has not yet been sent from heaven above
That truly captures the true depth of my love

Rush of Joy

With a smile in my soul I asked "do you want to?"
With a tear in her eye she answered "I do!"
The moment ignited into a feeling of bliss
As we treasured the moment with an euphoric ever-loving kiss

She asked "would the end be never?"
And I answered "that what is will be forever!"
And the moment became stronger
As another kiss made the feeling go on longer

And then in our eyes we each could see
That there were no more questions that needed to be
For with unspoken words from deep within our hearts
We swore to each other to never ever part

Through a Rainbow

She is letting me deeper and deeper into her soul
Giving more and more of her in whole
To depths she allows no one else to go
To be with the her that no one else will ever know

It is such a warm safe place to be
With so many wonderful things to see
It is like falling through a rainbow
That leaves your soul all aglow

It is truly such a feeling that I will always cherish
A soulful enrichment that will never perish
For the real her is truly a spectacular feeling to behold
That in my heart is a feeling that I will forever hold

Wildfire

At first it was all about just feeling her in my life
Then came the overwhelming need for her to be my wife
For what started out as just wanting her as a friend
Has become such a love that I never want to end

Amazing how it all happened in a blink of an eye
This feeling that without her I just want to die
All giving me a feeling of such sweet bliss
As she touched the depths of my soul with each and every hug and kiss

And as each moment passed I just found myself wanting her more
As each moment became so much more wonderful than the moment before
For all that she gave and gives is all that I will ever desire
From a love that burns through my soul like a raging wildfire

Like a Dream

What a special little girl
Sends my feelings into a whirl
So much life in her and so much more
So much of every bit of her do I adore

It is like burning from one feeling of love to another
Each being stronger and grander than the other
Taking my feelings to the utmost extreme
Making my whole life feel like a dream

All such a wonderful experience of which to be a part
With each passionate feeling going straight to my heart
Taking my soul where I never thought it could go
To know of love what I now want always and forever to know

Eternal Love

My life now feels so brand new
As fresh as the morning dew
All of a sudden it is like walking on air
As if I no longer having any crosses to bear

Such a feeling that it now makes me feel whole
Brings a whole new joy to the depths of my soul
All feeling so amazingly intense
As it all maxes out my each and every sense

For I now know I will no longer feel lonely again
Not like I did way back when
For right in the middle of everything I was not sure of
My love and I today professed the eternalness of our love

Serenity

We lie together
With the feeling of forever
With me in her arms and her in mine
Just enjoying how everything feels so divine

Such a special feeling as time slowly passes by
Makes us both feel like we could fly
As we just so silently lie there
Feeling how much for each other we really care

And as we both fade off to sleep
Knowing in our hearts this is forever ours to keep
We become engulfed by the feeling of serenity
From being where we always and forever want to be

Worth Waiting

For her I might have to wait years
Might have to cry a thousand million tears
For we are so in love with all of our hearts
But so far and a lifetime apart

Wish so much there was a way
To change being so far away
For the anguish of not being there
Has made it all so unbearable here

So sad that we love each other so much
And cannot even find a way to touch
But as much as all of this that I really hate
I know that if I have to wait forever and ever for her it will be so
      worth the wait

Shades of Pink

There is a girl I know
Who shies away from wearing a bow
Who is not much into wearing a girly skirt
Who would just rather wear her worn out jeans and her favorite
    throw-on shirt

She is someone who is not much into styling her hair
No pretty makeup for those who stare
Has no problem climbing a tree
Or being just the way she thinks she should be

She is more like a tomboy that is true
In just about everything that she does do
Except when it comes to being with me
Where the woman that she really is deep down inside she allows
    herself to be

The Thought of You

I thought about you again today
And it once again took all of my breath away
For within the simple thought of you
I always find the reason for everything within me to feel invigorated
      and new

So powerful is it that it makes me wish for nothing more
So wonderful that it makes my soul once again soar
Which is so hard to explain
How from it so many euphoric feelings remain

And forever will it be
That I want to have and embrace the thought of you and me
For you are the joy that I forever want within my mind
All the happiness within my heart that I ever want to find

Wonderful Love

There is a love
That I am so very sure of
That makes me complete
That I embrace in each and every heartbeat

It is felt so deep
And meant to keep
So precious and true
Meant for just two

Such a blessing to be
To all that can see
What you and I share
This love so rare

So Deep Asleep

In the middle of the night
When the stars are shining bright
I am able to so peacefully sleep
With the thoughts and feelings of her within me so deep

It is like a nightlight making me feel so at ease
As calm as a soft spring breeze
As her love for me engulfs all that I feel
Surrounding me with protecting emotional walls of steel

And as the night so silently slips by
As I lay under the moonlit sky
I let myself fade away so deeply into all of what she causes to be
Into the tranquility of everything she so lovingly feels for me

All of Me

She takes my breath away
Controls every word I say
Is master over everything I need
Is the blood that my heart does bleed

Such a joy being in her control
Of which I give to her in whole
For everything I want she gives
Deep within her is where my happiness lives

And it will always be until I no longer exist
That her power over me I will not be able to resist
For I will always want it to be
That I will always give her all of me

Promises

We each have said each and every word
That we made sure the other unconditionally heard
Where we made sure we were perfectly clear
That we both want to forever be with each other here

It is a promise that we made
Even though we were both afraid
As we both knew that this love was right
That with each other everything would be alright

And as with some promises that are spoken
This promise will never be broken
For there are just some things you should never say or start
Unless you really mean it with all of your heart

In Massive Awe

There is no living without each other now
Every bit of us is wrapped up around each other somehow
From the way our love will not perish
To the way it makes us feel that we now so whole-heartedly cherish

It is a feeling that we carry with us everywhere we go
Blinding us from all else that we may come to know
Making us feel like we are a million miles tall
Like we are both safely surrounded within each other's loving awe

All from the intense feelings over which we have no control
To the belief that we are now of one soul
As we both follow as the other one leads
To the love and companionship that now fulfills all of our needs

Such a Woman

My baby is the best
Better than all of the rest
No one here to compare
Her wonderful presence in life so very rare

She is truly such a treasure
Just the thought of her brings so much pleasure
So desirable in so many ways
A pure beauty to the eye always

Cannot begin to express her worth
Such a joy right from the very moment of her birth
For as a woman she does all that she can
To bring out the very essence of what makes me a man

Beyond Heartbreak

When love goes astray
We tend for a moment to lose our way
Between what was and what has become
From all that was anticipated but did not come

Such deep pain is this
To feel so deep the fall from bliss
From all that we have come to know
That was once the source of our euphoric glow

Just so agonizing which leaves us in despair
Of no longer feeling love and care
As we somehow find the strength within
To accept that this is where what is right for us has a chance to begin

No Cure

For her there is no cure
Each day I need her more and more
Just the desire of feeling her hug
Is like being addicted to a drug

Makes every moment away from her so very tough
Such a feeling that even when I am with her I cannot get enough
It is such a high that I do not want to ever come down from
A need that I will never try to overcome

It is something that only she can do
Who gives me this feeling of feeling brand new
From being the one whom she cares so much about
That I now cannot live without

Back to Her

So many unbearable moments without her now
That I must struggle through somehow
With so many feelings that I must now control
Just to make sure I do not lose the hope within my soul

Truth is that everything just seems to be in the way
Of being with her each and every day
All being so insignificant and without value
In place of a love that to me is so pure and true

But I know that I must be strong
To persevere through the moments being so long
For everything I do only leads back to what I so desire
To the one whom I so loving admire

Within Forever

There is a time between now and the end
Where I will be together with a godsend
Where she will call me husband and I her wife
Where we will share our love for each other for the rest of our life

It will be a moment of celebration and bliss
Entangled in emotions that will be sealed with a kiss
As we take each other into our waiting and wanting arms
Where we will protect each other from all of life's harms

And I know in my heart that this is where we were meant to be
Together as one just her and me
To never part no matter whatsoever
To live happily ever after within the promise of forever

A Wonderful Thing

I know it is going to be a wonderful thing
Such a feeling will it bring
This simple little touch
That will never be something that will ever be too much

It is something that I have waited for for so long
Something that I yearned for all along
As each moment which led to another
Was that much stronger than the other

But it is all worth waiting for
As I know that of it I will want so many more
As I know there is nothing more special than this
Than the feeling I will get from her deep passionate kiss

Children Playing

I wish so much we were childhood sweethearts
In love with each other right from the start
Growing up hand in hand
As we made our little castles in the sand

It would have been so wonderful to push you on the swing
Or to catch for you the carousel ring
Or laugh together as we made our way through the county fair
As I won for you the big stuffed animal from playing the games there

And as we grew
More into the one from the two
Our life would have been filled with the memories of a childhood
      love
That all of the rest of our lives would have been made up of

Unconquerably One

In so deep
Together forever to keep
For we have given ourselves to each other in whole
From the joy of our body to the depth of our soul

Such a wonderful feeling to be together by choice
Gives us so many reasons to rejoice
That saves us from falling into an emotional abyss
Of not feeling this feeling that immerses us both in bliss

All so very breathtaking in every way
As we both vow in every word we say
To never let this ever be undone
This feeling of now being soulfully one

Empathic

We feel deep
Feelings felt even while we sleep
For we listen to every word that is spoken
Suffer dearly whenever a promise is broken

Nothing is too small
So often do we need to withdraw
As everything is an emotional rush
Even feel the heaviness of a hush

We treat everyone as sister and brother
As we see with the eyes listen with the ears of another
To all beings we give of ourselves everything
For we are the true feelings of every living being

Breathing into You

I breathe into you words of love
As pure as if spoken by an angel from above
So you may feel so deep in your heart your soul in you
A love so rare and so true

There at the very depth of all that we are to be
Each word will echo throughout eternity
Filling us with tranquil feelings of peace
From a feeling that this true love will never cease

Joyfully this will be the essence of our fate
For the words will flourish and resonate
Where within the energy of each our love will flow
From which has become the breath of us so long ago

On My Way (to me)

I am taking a different path
Beyond this day of wrath
Where I decide what is right for me and what is wrong
For I am brave and I am strong

And on this day I shed all of the negative energy
So the positive may have the chance to be
Where I am letting go of the old
So all of the new may unfold

Yes, it is a new day
And I will make my way
To that which is good for my heart my soul my mind
Never again to let it be that of which I leave behind

Beyond Unsure

There was a moment before
When everything about us was so unsure
Where we felt each other out
To somehow see what we were all about

Then there came the moment after
That was so full of joy and laughter
Where everything about us was so sure
Which made us want each other just that much more

Now there is now
Where we feel as one within a love vow
As we can feel our love transcend
Beyond all that has a beginning and an end

Your Touch

You touched me
In places I never thought could be
That stirred the deepest part
Of everything I feel within my heart

You touched me again
In a way that only you can
Which made me crazed with need
To follow your each and every lead

You touched me once more and then more and more
So much that I long not for what was before
As I madly craved all so much
To feel only the amazing sensations of your each and every touch

Upon My Love

In your presence I fall to my knees
Do for you as you please
Give to you my wish upon a star
Worship you as the goddess that you are

For you are so amazing and truly magnificent in all ways
Worthy of so much more than just my admiration and praise
Exceptional through and through and to the core
Everything wonderful and so much more

Just all so breathtaking and undeniable
How I find you so incomparable
And while I know it is a little scary for you to be so high upon a pedestal
It is the strength of my love for you that will never let you fall

Adoring Awe

You I adore
Of which I want of you so much more
To fill my each and every night
To be the only one I see at the break of light

The mere thought of you
Makes me feel so brand new
Enriching my heart my soul
Bringing all the pieces of me together into making me whole

So much that I tremble inside
Feel my every sense amplified
As I embrace all that I feel
From within an awe of you that is just so beautifully surreal

Within the Space Between

From across the space between us we felt each other's touch
Through all else that did not matter all that much
As it all dissolved into a haze
On the periphery of our intense gaze

It all was such a moment of pure bliss
As magnificent as being locked in a passionate kiss
As we both could feel that forever us had just begun
From within this penetrating moment of us as one

Just so amazing how we filled each other's sight
How the deep connection felt so right
Where there was the feeling of only just us two
Captured in love within the space between me and you

Light Within the Dark

To this space we are sent
With our heartfelt consent
In the form of a baby girl and baby boy
To spread our love and joy

It is what this space needs
Someone to offset the dark deeds
Of those not from where we came
Who bring upon this space unspeakable shame

Of this we have no fear
For we know deep down why we are here
Of which we whole heartedly embrace
As the presence of light within this space

So in Love

What do I need to do
For there to be me and you
Just tell me
And with all of me I will make it be

This is not just something I say
Or words I use just to get us to lay
It is because without you with me I cry
Struggle from the feeling to just lie down and die

Of this don't think me as desperate and needy
That I lost all sense of reason and sanity
Don't even think me guided by forces from below or above
Think only of me as so in love

Ripped Clothes

Could hear the buttons hit the floor
As soon as we walked through the door
As she ripped the shirt from my back
Like some starved lioness on the attack

The moment just all so intense
As we could no longer withstand the suspense
Just had to have what the other wanted to give
As beyond this moment there was no other reason to live

Such a frenzy on the edge of insane
Like being engulfed by the strength of a hurricane
As the pure heated passion of fever ravished us to the very core
That left us both screaming for more

Muse

I am the poet
Because of the things I write and once wrote
Within me are the eloquent words that flow and rhyme
Which have been passed down from poet to poet over the ages of time

In being so I feel the darkness of midnight
And in turn express the magic in its moon's mysterious light
So as to open the mind of those who read each and every word
Quietly enlightening the heart of those like me who want to be heard

This is by far such a magnificent gift to be blessed with
To ink the words of love fantasy and enchanted myth
That so many embrace from within the depths of everything they hold true
That would have never been if not for the beautiful captivating inspiration of you

OTHER ANAPHORA LITERARY PRESS TITLES

The History of British and American Author-Publishers
By: Anna Faktorovich

Notes for Further Research
By: Molly Kirschner

The Encyclopedic Philosophy of Michel Serres
By: Keith Moser

The Visit
By: Michael G. Casey

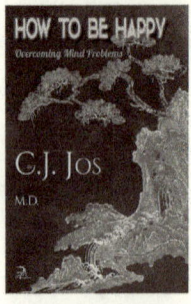

How to Be Happy
By: C. J. Jos

A Dying Breed
By: Scott Duff

Love in the Cretaceous
By: Howard W. Robertson

The Second of Seven
By: Jeremie Guy

www.ingramcontent.com/pod-product-compliance
Lightning Source LLC
Chambersburg PA
CBHW031135160426
43193CB00008B/145